D1472989

Sincerely Yours

Sincerely Yours

HOW TO WRITE GREAT LETTERS

by Elizabeth James & Carol Barkin

CLARION BOOKS · NEW YORK

11K3

Clarion Books
a Houghton Mifflin Company imprint
215 Park Avenue South, New York, NY 10003
Text copyright © 1993 by Elizabeth James and Carol Barkin

Library of Congress Cataloging-in-Publication Data
James, Elizabeth.
    Sincerely yours : how to write great letters / by Elizabeth James
and Carol Barkin.
        p. cm.
    Summary: Discusses the general purposes of writing letters and
outlines the elements of different types of personal and business
letters. Includes information on state abbreviations, forms of
address, and pen pals.
    ISBN 0-395-58831-6 (cloth). — ISBN 0-395-58832-4 (paper)
    1. Letter-writing—Juvenile literature.   [1. Letter writing.]
I. Barkin, Carol.   II. Title.
PE1483.J33   1993
808.6—dc20   91-42374
                              CIP
                               AC

AGM 10 9 8 7 6 5 4 3 2 1

In memory of Barbara Karlin—
a loving friend who embraced life with courage and joy,
and a lifelong advocate of excellence in books for children

Contents ॐ

Dear Reader ... ॐ

Don't you wish it were easier to think up what to say in those thank-you notes your parents make you write? Wouldn't you like to know that your friend who's away at camp can't wait to read your next letter? Does the fan mail you write to your favorite ball player or movie star sound boring and dumb? This book is the place to look for help.

There are lots of reasons to write letters. Personal letters help you keep in touch with people you know and care for. Thank-yous for gifts and special favors are more meaningful when they're written in a letter that the person can keep and reread. Letters to people you miss keep a friendship going when you're miles apart. A short note of apology to the neighbors whose window you broke playing baseball will make you more welcome next time you see them.

Business letters give you the opportunity to communicate with people you've never met. Complaints and requests for information get passed on to the right person just the way you wrote them; what you want doesn't get garbled, the way it can with phone messages. Writing an opinion letter gives you time to think through your ideas and express your views clearly.

Whether you're sending away for free stuff or telling Grandma about your new puppy or complaining to the school principal about a rule you think is unfair, well-written letters are the most effective way to communicate.

It's easy to learn to write good letters. And the best part is, the more letters you write, the better you get at writing them. If you're someone whose stomach tightens when you're faced with a box of stationery or whose fingers freeze on the computer keyboard when you type "Dear Aunt Mary," don't give up. Just try some of the ideas you'll find here, and before long you'll be writing lots of great letters — and your mailbox will be full of replies.

I. Personal Letters ॐ

Most letters fall into two main groups: personal letters and business letters. As you might guess, personal letters are the ones you write to people you know. You write to your family when you go away or when a family member is out of town. For instance, if your older sister has gone away to college, she'd love to have news from you about the neighborhood. You might write to your best friend when you're away at camp or on a trip.

Of course, relatives and friends who don't live nearby also love to keep in touch by mail. Grandparents, aunts and uncles, and cousins want to know what's new in your life and how the rest of the family is doing. A friend who has moved away will be happy to hear what's going on at your school.

Lots of people like to send cute or clever greeting cards instead of notes. Cards are fun to send and to receive, but a letter you write yourself is much more personal. It also costs less — cards are pretty expensive. And even when you do send a card, you'll want to add some words of your own.

How Should a Personal Letter Look?

A letter that can't be read by the person who receives it isn't much good, so the most important thing to remember is that your letters must be legible! Write carefully, especially if your handwriting is often a bit messy. Use a pen instead of a pencil, because pencil writing can smudge when your letter is handled.

If you know how to type, you can use a typewriter or computer for your letters. It used to be considered impolite to type a personal letter, but that's not true anymore. Maybe that's because typewriters and word processors are more common now than they used to be, and typing is more readable than most people's handwriting. An advantage of writing letters on a word processor is that making corrections and changes is so easy. And it's a great way to practice your typing skills.

Leaving margins (blank space between the writing and the edges of the paper) also helps make your letters easy to read. The margins form a frame around the writing that sets it off as it is read. So don't fill up every available blank area of your stationery — leave at least half an inch at the sides and enough space at the top and bottom so the letter looks nice.

Basics of a Personal Letter

Since personal letters are written to people you know, you don't need to put a whole lot of information at the top of your letter. It's not necessary to write your own address (called a return address) at the top of the first page as you

PERSONAL LETTER

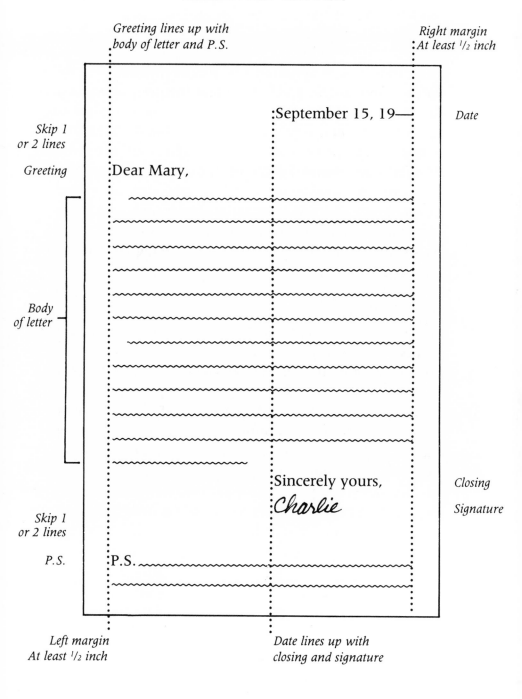

do in a business letter. Usually your friends and relatives already know where you live.

DATE

One thing that is important to put on all letters is the date — month, day, and year. It tells the person receiving the letter when you wrote it, even if it took a while to reach him or her. And for friends and family who keep letters to read again and again, the date your letter was written is an essential piece of information. Not putting the date on your letter would be like putting photos in an album and not identifying where and when they were taken. In a personal letter, the date is written at the upper right of the first page, a line or two higher than the greeting.

GREETING

Of course, every letter has to start with something. The words you use at the beginning of a letter are called the greeting or salutation. In personal letters your greeting can be the standard "Dear Susie" or something more informal. You might start your letters to friends from camp with "Greetings from Camp Confusion!" Or if you're spending a week at a dude ranch, you could start a letter by writing "Howdy, Aunt Jane." In personal letters, the greeting is usually followed by a comma, although it's fine to use an exclamation point or a dash for casual or funny greetings. Start the greeting at the left edge of the letter-writing space — don't indent it like a paragraph.

PAGE NUMBERS

If your letter is more than one page long, be sure to number every page after the first one. Just think how weird your letter would sound if your pal dropped the pages and then shuffled them back together wrong. If you were telling how much fun it was to learn to ride a horse at the end of page one, and then the next page started in the middle of a sentence about the shopping mall, your friend would think you'd lost your mind! So give your reader a clue by putting numbers on your letter pages. The upper right corner and the bottom center are both good places for page numbers.

CLOSING

At the end of your letter, you can just sign your name, but that might sound a little abrupt. It's customary to put a phrase called a closing, followed by a comma, before your signature. Some often-used closings are "Sincerely yours," "Yours truly," and "Love." But there are lots of other choices. For family members you might say something like "Your loving granddaughter" or "Your baseball-fan nephew." If you're bored with just plain "Love," you could vary it with "Love and kisses," "Lots of love," or "With love." Some people like to close with "Your friend."

But why not be creative? There are lots of well-known funny closings, like "Yours till Niagara Falls" and "Yours till the cookie crumbles." You can make up your own silly closings to amaze your friends.

In a personal letter, the closing is written below the letter itself and to the right, lined up with the date; the signature goes right underneath the closing.

P.S.

What does P.S. mean, anyway? Those two letters stand for the word "postscript," which comes from Latin words that mean "written afterward." Long ago, when everything was written by hand, people didn't want to have to rewrite a whole letter just because they left out one little fact. So they added a P.S. after they'd signed the letter to indicate that this was information they'd forgotten to include earlier.

If you think through what you plan to say in your letter before you start writing, you probably won't need to add a P.S. And if you're doing your letter on a computer, you'll be able to read it through and fix anything that's left out before you print it.

But maybe you've finished your letter and it's signed and ready to put into the envelope when you learn some news. That's the perfect time for a P.S. What if you wrote to your uncle about your book report and then you found out you got an A on it? Adding a P.S. to your letter to him will tell him the happy ending. Or perhaps you heard that your friend's hockey team won their game right before you put your letter to him in the mail. Of course you'll want to add "P.S. Congratulations on beating Lakewood!" to the bottom of your letter.

Line up your P.S. with the left edge of the letter, and start it a line or two below your signature.

Make Sure It Gets There

Millions of letters are mailed every day, so it's important to do what you can to make sure yours gets where it's going.

You probably already know that the stamp goes in the upper right corner of the envelope.

The address you're sending your letter to should be more or less centered, or slightly to the right, on the front of the envelope. The U.S. Postal Service says the address must all be written at least one inch in from the side edges; the first line of the address should be no more than $2^{3}/_{4}$ inches up from the bottom edge and the last line of the address should be at least $^{5}/_{8}$ inch up from the bottom. These rules are to allow the scanning machines to read addresses more easily.

Don't give the Postal Service any excuses to misdirect your letter. Write, print, or type clearly. The first line of the address should tell the name of the person you're writing to. The second line should contain the delivery address; be sure to include as much information as you have, such as apartment number, whether it's North Main Street or South Main Street, and so on. The third line should contain only the city, state, and ZIP code. (If you are mailing a letter to a foreign country, put the country name in capital letters on the fourth line.) Use standard state abbreviations without periods (see page 153). You can look up ZIP codes in the directory at any post office. If you know the four-number extension for the ZIP code, that's even better. It will help speed your letter on its way.

If you're writing to someone who is staying at another person's home or at a hotel, insert an extra line after the first one to include this extra information. This extra line might say "c/o Mrs. Hubbard" or "c/o Haystack Hotel" (c/o means "in care of").

Your return address (your name, street address, and city-state-ZIP) should go in the upper left corner of the envelope. Some people prefer to put the return address on

ENVELOPE

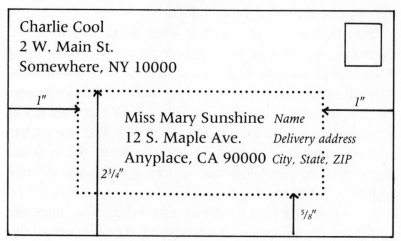

Return address — Charlie Cool / 2 W. Main St. / Somewhere, NY 10000 — *Stamp*

1" ↓   ✕ ....   1"

Miss Mary Sunshine *Name*
12 S. Maple Ave. *Delivery address*
Anyplace, CA 90000 *City, State, ZIP*

2³⁄₄"

⁵⁄₈"

Address should be inside dotted lines

the back flap, but it's easier to see on the front, and that's where the Postal Service wants it.

Putting your return address on the envelope is important. For one thing, if the person you're writing to has lost your address, he or she can copy it from your envelope. Also, if you forget to put on a stamp or if the letter can't be delivered for some other reason, the return address allows the Postal Service to return your letter to you.

When there is no return address on an undeliverable envelope, the Postal Service people open it to see if they can find the sender's address on whatever is inside. Then they send it back so you can start over with a new envelope and a new stamp. But if there's no way for anyone to figure out your address, your letter will probably wind up in the Dead Letter Branch. The Postal Service used to deliver unstamped mail, hoping that the person receiving the letter would pay for the stamp, but it doesn't always do that anymore.

FAX Facts

FAXes are fun to send and fun to receive. But it costs a lot of money both to send and to receive a FAX at a public FAX center; make sure the person you're sending a FAX to is willing to pay to get it. If you are allowed to use your family's FAX machine now and then, remember that sending a FAX costs the amount of a phone call to wherever it's going. Each FAX machine works a bit differently, so follow the instructions for the one you're using. And even though you don't use an envelope with a FAX, you need to put your own FAX number on your message as well as the number it's going to.

Free Stamps

Sometimes you'll find stamps that have been stuck to an envelope but haven't been used. If the stamp has no cancellation (the part of the postmark inked across the stamp to show it's been used), you are free to use it yourself.

If you have an uncanceled stamp that you can't peel off the envelope, there's an easy way to unglue it. Tear off the whole corner of the envelope, including the stamp. Soak the envelope corner in lukewarm water for a while. Pretty soon the stamp will just slide off the paper it's stuck to. Dry the stamp facedown on a sink counter or a paper towel; then use white glue or rubber cement to stick it to a new envelope. (Don't use tape, because the stamp can't be canceled through it.)

Envelope Decoration

It's a good idea to keep the front of an envelope clean except for the stamp, the name and address it's going to, and your return address. Putting a lot of goofy stuff on the front of an envelope may make the address hard to read and the letter hard to deliver. But you can always decorate the envelope's back. It's fun to do and makes your letters shout that they're from you even before they're opened.

If you're good at drawing, you might want to add a picture to the back of your envelope. It can be anything you like — a field of flowers, your new cat, or birds on the wing. But even not-so-great artists can usually draw cartoons. Make one, two, or three frames showing something that happened to you at home, school, or camp. Stick figures are fine; add balloons for words or thoughts to tell what's going on.

Using rubber stamps and different-colored ink pads is another great way to decorate the backs of your envelopes. Stickers are also perfect to put on envelope backs, and you may not need to buy them. Lots of charities, such as the National Wildlife Federation, send free picture stamps with their letters asking for donations. Most adults don't bother putting them on their personal letters, and they're not appropriate for business correspondence. So if there aren't any at your house, ask around. A neighbor may be happy to save some for you next time they come in the mail.

You can use these stamps the way they are or you can cut parts of them out and make whole scenes. But be careful to stick them down tight, without overlapping. If the outside of your envelope is all lumpy, it might get damaged going through the mail-sorting machines.

Not-So-Secret Messages

There are lots of times you might want or need to write something on the back of an envelope you're sending. Maybe you just found out something that you would have put in a P.S. but the envelope was already sealed. A short note is fine to put on the back of an envelope. Just remember that what you say can be read by anyone who handles the mail — so why not keep it secret?

An age-old "secret" message to write on the flap of an envelope is S.W.A.K. — it stands for "sealed with a kiss." Sticking on the postage stamp upside down is another way of secretly sending a love message through the mail, and the Postal Service doesn't care which way the stamp is stuck on as long as it has the correct money value. But most people know what these messages stand for, so use secret code on your envelopes instead and keep your messages really private.

There are lots of books on how to write coded messages, but here are a few ideas to get you started. Backward code, in which you write what you want to say using the last letter first and so on, is easy to do, but it's also easy to figure out. Why not use something trickier, like a backward alphabet-substitution code, where a = z, b = y, x = c, etc.? Or you could even substitute numbers for letters of the alphabet, where 1 = a, 2 = b, 3 = c, etc., and write your messages that way. (Remember to put a dash between the numbers so your friend will know you mean 2-1-25 for "bay" and not 2-1-2-5 for "babe.")

Just be sure that whatever code you use, you and your friend agree on it ahead of time. There's not much point in a message so secret that only you can read it!

Personalizing Stationery

Of course the important part of your letter is what you write. But lots of people like using stationery that expresses their individuality. It's easy to find decorative stationery and envelope sets to buy. Pads of paper come with all sorts of designs, and some places will even print your first name on every page of a pad. However, you might decide that designer stationery is too expensive, or you might not find a look you like. If so, why not make your own?

The first step in making your own stationery is to choose paper that is the right size to fit in the envelopes you plan to use. Packages of inexpensive correspondence envelopes come in two sizes — $6\frac{1}{2}'' \times 3\frac{5}{8}''$ Commercial size and $9\frac{1}{2}'' \times 4\frac{1}{8}''$ Standard size.

The paper on inexpensive $6'' \times 9''$ pads, folded in thirds, fits in a Commercial envelope. If you use regular $8\frac{1}{2}'' \times 11''$ paper, such as typing paper or notebook paper, it can easily be folded in thirds to fit the larger Standard envelope or in half and then in thirds to fit the smaller Commercial size. Using paper and envelopes in sizes other than these common ones is usually more trouble than it's worth. (The Postal Service will not accept envelopes smaller than $3\frac{1}{2}'' \times 5''$.)

Look for colored paper if you don't want plain white; try a copying store or a print shop. You might even want to cut the paper into a simple design, like a circle or a heart or a silhouetted face in profile. If you start out with standard-size paper, you know that your shaped stationery will fit into your envelopes. Make a pattern and use it to cut several sheets at one time.

You can decorate your stationery any way you like, either by drawing on each piece or by using rubber stamps and stickers. One way to make a lot of stationery is to draw a design on one sheet and then have it run off on a copier. It's best to draw the design on a plain white sheet of paper, even if you plan to have it copied onto colored paper. Draw your design in black ink, because other colors often don't copy well.

While paying by the sheet at a coin-operated copying machine is probably too expensive, you may know someone who has a copy machine or access to one at work. Ask if he or she would mind running off a dozen or so copies of your personalized stationery for free or very low cost — you'll probably need to supply the paper, though, especially if you want to use colored sheets.

If you're having stationery copied on a machine, it's a good idea to print or type your name and address at the top of the sheet. While it's not necessary to put a return address on personal letters, it is handy to have it there so that the person you write to won't have to look it up. You could make an elegant or funny design around your name and address, but do make sure that the numbers and words are easy to read. Use the sheets with your return address on them only for the first page of a letter.

You can't copy onto paper that's already been cut into a design, but you can always draw the shape you want to cut, decorate it, and make copies. Then cut the printed sheets into the shape you've drawn.

Hint: If you find it hard to keep your writing straight on unlined paper, try putting a sheet of lined paper under your stationery. If the lines are dark enough, they'll show faintly through the stationery and you can use them as a guide.

Personalized Postcards

Postcards are cheaper to use than stationery because they need less postage and don't need envelopes. But, just like messages on the backs of envelopes, anything you write on a postcard can be read by anyone who handles it. Still, postcards are fun to decorate and send, and if you don't have much to say, their small writing space is perfect.

You can buy "free" postcards at the post office. They cost only the amount of the postage that's printed on them, but they're pretty boring to look at. One side has the stamp and room to write the address, and the other is blank for your message.

While it's never a good idea to wildly decorate the space around the address or stamp (you don't want to confuse the Postal Service and have your card lost), you can certainly jazz up the message side. Even a colorful border of curlicues will liven up these plain postcards and still leave plenty of room for you to write a few lines.

Or you can make your own postcards. (The smallest postcard the Postal Service will accept is $3\frac{1}{2}'' \times 5''$; the biggest size you can send with postcard postage is $4\frac{1}{4}'' \times 6''$.) For handmade postcards you'll need paper that's stiff enough to go through the mail without being ripped to shreds. Most copy and print shops sell card stock in lots of pretty colors. Card stock comes in $8\frac{1}{2}'' \times 11''$ sheets. If you ask the clerk at the copy shop to cut your card stock into quarters with a paper cutter, you'll end up with cards that can be mailed at the postcard rate. For a glamorous effect, use a contrasting-color pen to draw a design and write your message.

Another great do-it-yourself postcard is a regular snapshot (just be sure it fits into the Postal Service's size guidelines). Maybe you have photos of yourself winning the blue ribbon at the county fair. Your aunt who taught you to grow those prize-winning vegetables will be thrilled to get this picture postcard with just a short note on the back. And if someone in your family takes photos of just about everything and no one knows what to do with all the extras that won't fit into an album, using them as postcards will make everyone happy.

The only problem with using photos as postcards is that the slippery paper they are printed on may make your writing smear. So use ballpoint pen, and check to make sure it's not smearing before you write the whole message and address. Another method is to use plain self-stick labels; if you cover the back of the photo with labels, you'll have a much better surface to write on. Draw a line down the middle of the back of the snapshot and use the right-hand side for the address. Now you've got a fabulous picture postcard to send off.

Just remember that whatever you do about stationery and envelopes or postcards, the important part is your message to your friend or relative. Your homesick pal who's moved away or your favorite aunt will be happy to hear from you no matter what you write your letter on.

1. Saying Hi by Mail ৶

One reason you might put off writing personal letters is that you don't feel you know what to say. But it's easier than you think. All you need to do is write the way you talk, only taking out all the "uhs" and pauses. In a personal letter, be as chatty and natural as you can. After all, whoever you're writing to knows you and wants to feel that he or she can almost hear you talking. So pretend you're having a conversation with that person.

What would the two of you talk about together? If you're writing back to someone who wrote to you, take a moment to look over the letter you received. There are probably some questions in it that you want to answer or something your friend said that you'd like to comment on. And be sure to ask some questions yourself; they make a good starting point for a letter back to you.

Letters aren't only about events. Try to express your feelings too. You're not writing a news report that gives only the bare facts. You're telling someone your own point of view—your thoughts and emotions and your reactions to things that happen.

When you're deciding what to say in your personal

letters, think about how you feel when you open a letter yourself. What questions are running through your mind? Are you wondering if your cousin got chosen for the team? Are you hoping your big sister will tell you what it's really like to live in a college dorm? Do you want to find out whether your best friend from camp is going to be there again this summer?

Now try to put yourself in the place of the person you're writing to. What will she be wondering when she opens your letter? Did you answer her questions and ask a few of your own? After all, the main reason to write personal letters is to keep in touch with people we don't see every day. So share some secrets, pass along some jokes, and put some of your everyday life into your letters.

Keeping in Touch with Friends

When a friend moves away, it's lonely for both of you. While he is surrounded by unfamiliar faces, you are still hanging around the same old places being reminded all the time that your friend isn't there to share the fun with you. Both of you will eventually find new friends. But that doesn't need to change the feelings you and your old friend have for each other.

Let your friend know how much you miss him. You might tell him you hope he's having fun in his new town, but you miss doing the things you used to do together. Be specific. Remember when the two of you went fishing and he was the only person in the world who saw that huge fish you caught before it got away? That's a memory only the two of you can share.

Letters between friends keep a friendship growing. They

give you a chance to find out about your pal's room in her new home and what the kids in her new school are like. They give her a chance to hear what's going on with the people and places she's left behind. Maybe through your letters you'll be able to plan to go to the same camp next summer or visit each other during a school break. And of course, if you're the one who moved away, letters will remind you that your old friendships are still special.

Here's what Charlie Cool wrote to his friend Kevin, who had just moved to another part of the state.

June 25, 19—

Dear Kevin,

How ya doin'? It's weird that you're not around anymore. We're still playing baseball here, and I keep thinking you're over there at first base waiting for my throw. Donny Jenkins is playing first base now, and he's not as good as you. But we beat Springtown last week, and they've got a great pitcher, so we felt pretty good. Are you going to join a team up there?

One thing I have to tell you is that Mr. Schmidt is getting married to a teacher from another school. Can you believe it? He's a lot nicer than he used to be. Also, Jim and Terry got in a big fight after a game and got suspended for two days.

What are you doing on the Fourth of July? Linda Gordon is having a big party and my whole family is invited, so I guess I'll go. Then we're going to watch the fireworks down at the park — remember last year when we snuck up behind Jim and his brother and scared them?

We're going to Colorado in August for vacation. It should be pretty neat.

Hope you like your new house and everything, but not too much, if you know what I mean. Write back soon.

Gotta go,
Charlie C.

If you're separated from your friends for a shorter period of time — for instance, when you go away to camp or off to visit relatives for a week or two — take your stationery and address book with you. Even when you're having fun, you may still miss your friends. Sharing your adventures with them through letters is the next best thing to having them there with you. And they're more likely to write to you if you've already written to them.

Here's what Mary Sunshine wrote to her friend Lisa.

July 5, 19—

Dear Lisa,

I'm still at Aunt Janet's house, but we're coming home on Sunday. It's pretty much fun here — the people next door have a pool that we can use whenever we want. They had a great party in their backyard yesterday with a big barbecue and a ton of food. Two of their kids are a lot younger than me, and they also have a son in college. So sometimes I've baby-sat with the little kids while their mom goes to the store.

Aunt Janet keeps taking me to museums, but actually there were some terrific statues in one of them. What are you doing with yourself? Did you go anywhere for the Fourth of July? How are your tennis lessons coming along? I bet I can still beat you when I get home. Sign us up for a court on Monday so we can get in some games before I go. See you soon.

Miss you,
Mary

If you're the one who's home, remember that getting mail is really a treat for your friends who are away. They love to hear what everyone back home is doing and to know they haven't been forgotten just because they're out of town. So before you dash out the door or when you're almost ready for bed, take a few minutes to write all the news to a friend who's away from home.

Here's what Mary Sunshine wrote to her friend Ilene.

August 8, 19—

Dear Ilene,

Hope you're having fun up at your camp. It's been really hot here and I've been at the beach every day since I got back from my camp. But at least we don't have mosquitoes here. The ones you wrote about last time sounded like real killers! Actually, it's kind of boring right now because almost everybody is away. But Lisa and I played tennis the other day and we saw Holly afterward. She had this totally gorgeous guy with her who turned out to be her cousin who's visiting from Mississippi. He's going home tomorrow — too bad!

Guess what? Some people bought the Wilsons' old house and my mom heard that they've got a son who will be in our grade. They're not moving in until right before school starts, so I haven't seen him yet. I hope he doesn't turn out to be like Jason Wilson — do you think houses choose their owners or the other way around?

Anyway, have fun for the rest of camp and I'll see you when you get home.

Luvya,
Mary

When you're off on vacation with your family, it's often hard to find the time to write letters to your friends. But some postcards with a few lines scrawled on them let others know that while you're having fun, you're still thinking of them. Just as with any other kind of correspondence, you are more likely to get cards from traveling pals if you send some off yourself when you're away.

Here are some cards that Charlie Cool managed to write to friends while he and his family were traveling through the Rocky Mountains.

August 10, 19—

Hey, Roger!

Here we are on the top of the world, or at least it feels that way. We actually drove to the top of this mountain yesterday. Amazing! Hope you're having fun back home. See ya soon!

Charlie C.

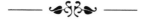

August 12, 19—

Hi, Jerry—

These mountains are so neat. Tomorrow we're going to pan for gold in an old creek near here — maybe I'll find a gold nugget! You won't believe this — we saw Linda and her uncle in Cripple Creek. Did you know she was going to be out here this summer?

See ya,
Charlie C.

What about your buddy who is in the hospital or is stuck at home because he's had an operation? He probably feels terrible being cooped up and he's got a lot of time to think about all the stuff he's missing. Your cards and letters will help him feel included and still part of your old gang. Maybe a bunch of you could write a group letter — one of you writes the first paragraph, another the next, and so forth. Or you could each jot down a short note and put them all in one big envelope to mail. Be sure to tell him the latest jokes and riddles that are going around and include trivia news to keep him up to date.

Here's what Charlie Cool and some of his friends wrote to a classmate who was in the hospital.

November 4, 19—

Dear Donny,

Sorry to hear you're still sick — I guess you won't be back at school for a while. Lucky you! You're missing a lot of really boring stuff. We had a test in math yesterday that was mucho tough. Do you have to take the tests in the hospital or what? I got a new hamster, and I'm going to teach it to play soccer with marbles (just kidding). Now it's Terry's turn to write. Get well soon.

Jim

Hi, Donny!

How's the food in the hospital? Better than the school lunchroom, I bet! You must be getting bored, but at least you can watch all the TV you want, right? I'm planning to have a party on my birthday next month — hope you'll be okay by then. We're going to a movie and then for pizza. Hope you feel better soon.

Terry

Hey Big Don —

I miss you in class — nobody to goof off with when you're not there! But I hear they're letting you go home soon, so I'll come and visit. Did you see the Giants game on TV? Incredible! I think you and me could do better, except my mom won't let me play football (joke). Terry didn't tell you, but he got in another fight — with Rick. You can probably guess that Terry has a black eye, plus detention again. See ya soon, I hope —

Charlie C.

If you have a pen pal, that's probably the person you write to most often. (If you don't have one but would like to, see page 161 for a list of pen pal organizations.) Letters to a pen pal are a bit different from those to your other friends. Your pen pal doesn't know anyone you do and has probably never seen where you live. You'll have to provide extra information to make sure your pen pal knows what you're talking about. But that gives you the opportunity to write great character sketches of your friends and family and descriptions of your hometown.

The other half of the fun is receiving letters from your pen pal. You'll get to know a new friend and find out about a whole new place. Many people have written to the same pen pal for years and have even arranged to meet in one or the other's home. Imagine going to Singapore or Argentina to meet the person you've become friends with by mail!

Here's what Mary Sunshine wrote to her pen pal, Emma Little, who lives in England.

November 10, 19—

Dear Emma,

Thanks for your letter. It was neat to hear all about Guy Fawkes Day. Here we're starting to get ready for Thanksgiving, which is in a couple of weeks — I know you don't celebrate it in England, but it's a big holiday here. We get two days off from school for it — hooray!

Mom is inviting practically the whole world for Thanksgiving at our house. My sister Anna is coming home from college and she's bringing her roommate Ellen who lives in New Jersey. Ellen thinks it will be weird, because it's always cold in New Jersey in November and sometimes there's even snow, but here in California it's warm and sunny like always.

Aunt Janet's coming too — remember I told you about her? She always brings some kind of food that the real Pilgrims ate, and this year it's going to be Indian pudding. Nobody but her knows what Indian pudding is. Last year she brought succotash (which is corn and lima beans mixed together, in case you don't have it in England). I hate lima beans, so I had to pick them all out before I could eat it. Anyway, my mom will probably make some pies, so we won't starve to death!

Write back soon!

Your pen pal,
Mary

Writing letters is a great way to keep in touch with friends. It doesn't take much time once you get started, and it gives both you and your friends a lot of pleasure.

2. The Family Connection ✒

Families in today's world seem to move around a lot, so you're likely to have relatives who don't see you very often. It's hard to feel close to them even though you're all part of the same family. Letters and short notes with photos keep family members connected, and that's important to all of you.

Older people in your family may be especially happy to hear from you. Do you have an aunt who lives alone? Letters from you will cheer her up if she's feeling lonely and will let her know she's not forgotten by her family.

Sometimes grandparents feel a little left out of their grandchildren's lives, and writing to them is an easy way to include them in your everyday doings. Most grandparents can't help feeling proud of their grandkids, and getting your letters gives them something extra to be proud of.

Let's pretend you're writing to your grandma. She probably wants to know how school is going — grandmothers usually do. And let's say that school is pretty boring right now and you don't have much to say about it. Does that mean you have nothing to write? Of course not. Think about what other things you do at school besides go to class. Grandma would be happy to know how you're doing in the sports program or to hear all about the weird thing that happened at band practice the other day. And you know she always wants news of your family — did your baby sister's new front tooth just come in? Did your mom get a promotion at work? Did your dad take a bunch of great photos of your family's new van? (Be sure to send her one.)

Think about the person you're writing to and what he or she would want to hear. For example, you probably don't need to tell Grandma all the details of the fight you got into after school when you ripped your shirt (although your cousin Roger might love to know all about it). This sort of news might make Grandma worry about you. On the other hand, there may be things you'd like to share with someone you don't see every day. If you've had a problem with a friend that's hard to talk over with your parents, Grandma might be the perfect person to write to. She'll be sympathetic and she may also have some good advice.

Here's what Mary Sunshine wrote to her grandparents in Seattle.

> December 4, 19—
>
> Dear Grandma and Grandpa,
>
> We really missed you at Thanksgiving. A whole bunch of people had dinner here, but it wasn't like last year when you came down for the weekend. Mom says you're feeling better, Grandpa, so I hope I'll get to see you soon.
>
> I can't remember if I told you I was trying out for the school play, but guess what — I got a part!

We're doing fairy tales set in modern times, and I'm going to be Cinderella's stepmother. I can't wait — I get to be as mean and nasty as I want! And the teacher says she'll do some really mean-looking makeup for me.

Anna was home for Thanksgiving with her roommate Ellen. Ellen is pretty nice, but Anna and I got in a big thing because I've been using her desk to do my homework. You know my room is so little I can't put a big desk in there, and I didn't think she'd mind and Mom thought it would be okay if I was careful. And I was! But Anna said I left all my school stuff in a mess on the desk (which wasn't true, it wasn't messy), and then she said I was borrowing stuff she didn't take to college. I was so mad at her! We sort of made up, but I still think she wasn't being fair. Why can't I use her room when she's not using it? Mom says maybe Anna's a little home-sick and she wants her room to be just like it always was, but I'm still upset. Oh, well, I guess it'll be okay.

Anyway, keep getting better, Grandpa. I love you both.

Love and kisses,
Mary

If your family is large, writing to everyone who lives far away may seem overwhelming. Of course, some families send photocopies of family news to the whole clan. You've probably seen these letters at Christmastime. Sending a photocopied letter is a great way to keep relatives and friends up to date without spending all your time writing the same news over and over again to different people. But some families find these letters, which are usually written by one parent, kind of impersonal.

You might get your family to write a different kind of letter to be copied and sent to aunts, uncles, and grandparents. Use one sheet of paper and ask each of your parents and brothers and sisters to write a short note on it (little kids can draw a picture or make a handprint with poster paint). Don't forget to write something yourself! Then make as many copies of the letter as you need and mail them off.

This kind of group letter is a great holiday greeting, and it's also terrific for birthdays. Instead of buying cards, you'll each be sending a personal "Happy Birthday" as well as news of the family.

Here's what Charlie Cool and his sister wrote as part of a family group letter to their great-aunt Alice, who lives in Massachusetts with their grandparents.

January 17, 19—

Dear Great-Aunt Alice,

Happy birthday! Hope you have a great special day. And I hope that you get lots of nice presents and that Nana and Gramps take you out for a nice birthday dinner. I can't wait to see you on the February vacation. Hope there's a lot of snow up there, because I want to use my new cross-country skis.

Happy birthday again. Love you.

Amanda

Happy Birthday, Great-Aunt Alice!

All those faces you see around the edge of this letter are all of us singing "Happy Birthday to You" (that's why they have little music notes around them). I heard on the news that there's a big snowstorm coming. Is Gramps's old sleigh still out in the barn? If it is, I'll give you a ride when we come up in February. I've got to sign off, because it's Mom and Dad's turn to write. We all sent you a present, but I can't tell you what it is — it's a surprise. Hope you like it.

> Love,
> Charlie

Do you have several cousins in different parts of the country? Here's a clever way for all of you to stay in touch: a family round-robin letter. Start by writing a letter to your cousins, and send it to one of them. Tell him to write his own letter and send both his letter and yours to the next cousin in line. The third cousin adds a letter and sends all three on to whoever is next.

Eventually all the letters will come back to you. You'll get to read through all the news from each person and their responses to the letters they received. Now it's your turn to write again. Remove your original letter, which everyone has read by this time; add your new letter to the collection, and send it all off to the next person on the list. Make sure all the letters are dated, so you'll all know who wrote what when.

A round robin like this can keep going as long as you want. It lets everyone share what's going on with the whole gang, but each of you has to write only one letter in each round. This kind of round-robin letter is also a great way to keep in touch with a bunch of friends over the summer.

Here's what Charlie Cool wrote in his part of a round-robin letter with his cousins.

February 7, 19—
Hey, Guys! (This means Drew, Brian, and Matt in case you didn't know!)

This is a great idea! I'd never have known what you all were up to if somebody hadn't started this letter. Well, I guess I'm supposed to tell you what's happening. Here goes. We're all going up to Massachusetts to my other grandparents' house for vacation in two weeks. It should be pretty much fun. The winter here has been really cold and we've had *two snow days*! My buddy Jim and I joined a hockey team — I'm pretty lousy, but it's fun. My mom's afraid I'll break my neck or my head, but so far all I did was bang my thumb against the boards — big deal. Maybe we can all play roller hockey this summer. By the way, Brian, hope your broken arm is getting better. What a drag.

School's okay. Math is still hard, but science is pretty neat. Well, gotta go finish my homework so I can watch the Knicks on TV.

Signing off,
Charlie C.

Another unusual way to keep in touch is a diary letter. This might be especially appropriate if one of your parents is away on a long business trip. He or she will know what you've been doing every day and will feel less lonely for home.

You don't need to use a real diary for this; any kind of stationery is fine. The idea is to spend a few minutes each night before you go to bed writing down what happened that day and how you felt about it. You don't have to write a lot each time, just enough to give the flavor of your daily life.

If your mom or dad is going to be away for a long time, mail your diary letter once a week. If you don't have an address to send it to, save it to be read when he or she gets home.

Of course you can send a diary letter to anyone you want. Other relatives would love to get one, and they'll be flattered that you wanted to send it. A diary letter from camp would be a lot of fun for your aunt who went to that same camp years ago, or for your friend who's spending the summer at home. And maybe she'll write one back to you.

Here's what Mary Sunshine wrote in part of her diary letter to her mom, who was up in Seattle helping Grandma take care of Grandpa.

February 26, 19—

Dear Mom,

I hope Grandpa is feeling better. I bet Grandma is glad he's home from the hospital, but I guess he's still pretty sick or you wouldn't be up there. We miss you a lot, but everything's fine. Is it raining in Seattle still?

February 27, 19—

Hi Mom,

Aunt Janet came for the weekend. She made dinner for us tonight. It was pretty weird, but actually it tasted okay. I got another letter from Emma. Do you think I could go to England and visit her sometime? Lisa and I went to the mall today — her mom took us and we had lunch at the Mexican place, the one I like so much. Bye for now.

February 28, 19—

Mom, how's Grandpa doing? You sounded funny on the phone tonight, like you were really sad. We miss you. Mark likes having Mrs. Wells come and baby-sit. She's pretty nice, but it's not the same as having you here. We're starting clay sculpture in art tomorrow — Dad gave me one of his old shirts to use as a smock. Talk to you soon.

Lots of love,
Mary

Whether you write a postcard or a five-page letter, friends and family will be happy to hear from you.

3. Thank-You Notes 🦢

Write a thank-you note? Yuk! It's so boring — do I have to?

Does that sound like something you might say? Most kids hate writing thank-you notes, and most parents have to nag their children to get them to sit down and do it. But why is that? What's so hard about writing a thank-you note?

Well, it's really not that it's so hard, right? It's that you don't know what to say, and all your thank-you notes sound the same ("Thank you for the wonderful . . . I like it a lot") and none of them sound like you. They all seem to turn out kind of stiff-sounding and — what's even worse — insincere. And that makes you think they're not worth writing, and that the people who receive them will think they're dumb.

But that's not true! Everyone — young or old, close friend or distant relative — likes to receive a thank-you note. Basically, a thank-you note is just ordinary good manners. It's a way of letting people know that you received their gift or appreciated the favor they did. When you stop to think about it, writing a short note is little enough to do for someone who took the trouble to give you a present or do something nice for you. From a purely selfish point of view, writing a thank-you note makes it more likely that that person will give you another gift or do you another favor later on. After all, if you don't let people know you appreciate their gifts, why should they bother giving you more?

Like any other kind of letter, a thank-you note is more permanent than a phone call. It can be reread by the person who receives it or passed around to other members of the family to be appreciated. A letter is more work for you than picking up the phone, and so it shows you feel grateful enough to take that trouble.

It's best to write a thank-you note as soon as possible after you receive the gift. Otherwise, you tend to keep putting it off, and after several weeks have passed, you feel too embarrassed to send it at all. Besides, if you wait for months to send a thank-you note, Aunt Mary may have forgotten what she sent you so long ago. In the meantime she's probably been wondering if you ever got her gift or feeling hurt that you never said thanks.

Thank-you notes don't have to be very long, but they should express your personality and your relationship to the person you're thanking. They can be funny or loving or just plain polite, depending on how you feel about the person you're writing to.

Make sure to mention specifically what you're saying thank you for — the football you've been wanting or the sweater that goes perfectly with your ski pants. If you just say "Thanks for the nice gift," that sounds as if you didn't care about it enough to remember what it was.

What if you don't really like the gift? You still need to

write a thank-you note. Remember that old saying, "It's the thought that counts." Maybe Uncle John and Aunt Mary have terrible taste in T-shirts or they gave you a book that would have been too easy for you in first grade. Still, they tried; they took the time and trouble to get you a gift, and certainly they hoped you would like it. You don't have to tell lies in your note — don't say "It's the nicest scarf I ever had" if you plan to hide it in your dresser drawer forever — but do say how much you appreciate their thoughtfulness.

Thank-Yous for Gifts

Anyone who gives you any kind of present deserves a thank-you note. So there you are at your desk with a list of the friends and relatives who gave you birthday gifts or holiday presents. Luckily, most of these people won't be comparing notes with one another, so you can write the same basic note to everyone, changing it to fit each person and the gift he or she gave you. Here's how.

Paragraph 1. Plunge right in — this is a thank-you note, so you should start by saying thank you. Mention the present specifically. Then go on to say something descriptive about the gift and why you like it. You can be as enthusiastic as you want. Remember that thank-you notes can be very informal and chatty. If you really love the gift, you might say:

Thank you, thank you, thank you for the gorgeous necklace — I love it!

Here are some hints for what to say about different kinds of gifts. For something handmade by the giver, mention how delicious (for food) or pretty (for clothes, etc.) or useful (for school stuff) it is, and how much you appreciate the person's time and effort in making it. If someone has given you tickets to a ball game or a play, be sure to mention something you especially enjoyed — the tie-breaking home run or the play's dramatic surprise ending or the chance to see one of your heroes in real life.

When someone has given you money, try to give some idea of how you plan to use it. People usually give money because they don't know what you want and they hope you'll use it for something special. You could mention that you're adding it to your savings for a new bike or that you'll spend it on a piece of clothing you've been wanting, or even that you plan to use it to take all your friends out for pizza for your birthday.

Notice that by this time you've already written two or three sentences; you don't need much more for this kind of note.

Paragraph 2. Here's where you say something nice about the person who sent the present. After all, it's that person's thoughtfulness that resulted in your receiving a gift. You might mention the person's special knowledge about whatever he or she gave you or say you appreciate his or her attention to your particular likes and dislikes. Or you can simply refer to the person's kindness or generosity in thinking of you. This paragraph needn't be long, but it's important because it lets the person who gave you a gift know that you appreciate him or her, and not just the present.

Paragraph 3. It never hurts to repeat your thanks at the conclusion of your note. You can vary the words a little; if you said "Thank you very much" at the beginning, try "Thanks again" or "Many thanks" at the end.

Now sign your name and you're finished. Pretty easy, wasn't it?

Here are thank-you notes Mary Sunshine and Charlie Cool wrote for birthday presents.

March 10, 19—

Dear Aunt Janet,

Thank you so much for the gift certificate to The Gazebo you sent me for my birthday. I haven't decided yet between a beautiful green sweater that would go with a lot of my skirts or a fabulous pants outfit I saw there yesterday. I'll let you know which one I end up getting.

I guess you figured out when you stayed with us that The Gazebo is absolutely my favorite store. You really are smart — no one else knew that a gift certificate there was what I wanted most. I'm sure glad I have you for an aunt.

Thanks again. Next time I see you I'll show you what I bought!

Love,
Mary

—— ✺ ——

March 17, 19—

Yo, Kev —

Thanks a lot for that Syracuse basketball jersey you sent me for my birthday. What a great surprise! I wore it to school today over my turtleneck and everybody wanted to know where I got it. I told them Syracuse was trying to sign me up (joke).

I sure wish you'd been here for my birthday, but getting the jersey and that funny card you sent was the next best thing. I shouldn't have been surprised that you remembered my birthday, though. After all, we've been friends since nursery school.

Thanks again. Hope we can get together before too long. Maybe we can work something out for this summer.

Your best buddy,
Charlie C.

Thank-Yous for Hospitality

A thank-you note you send to someone whose home you stayed in is called a bread-and-butter letter. People always like to hear that you had a good time while you were visiting them and that you are grateful for their hospitality.

If you go to stay with a friend's family in the country, you should write to your friend's parents or grandparents or whoever owns the house. You might also write a separate short note or a postcard of thanks to your friend. The same applies to visiting an old friend who has moved to another city; you must certainly write to your friend's parents to thank them for having you, and it's nice to write to your friend as well. An overnight (or longer) visit to a relative also deserves a thank-you note. Even if your whole family stayed at Great-Uncle Charlie's house for a family reunion, you can send your own thank-you note separately from the one your parents write; it will make Great-Uncle Charlie feel loved and appreciated.

Like other thank-you notes, a bread-and-butter letter

doesn't have to be very long, and it should follow a structure similar to the one for gift thank-yous.

Paragraph 1. Say thanks before you say anything else — that's the whole point of your note. Then refer to something that made your visit special. You might say something like:

Thanks a lot for letting the whole Johnson crew stay at your house for the big reunion. It was great to get a chance at last to sample Aunt Mabel's famous fritters — Dad's been telling me about them as long as I can remember, and everything he said was true. They were great!

Mentioning something special about your visit lets your hosts know that you have happy memories of your stay with them.

Paragraph 2. This is the time to tell your hosts how kind they were to invite you to their house, to include you in their plans while you were there, to take the extra trouble to make your visit fun, or just to make you feel at home. You might say:

When I realized that you'd baked my favorite chocolate cake for the first night I was there, I felt truly welcome.

This tells your hosts that you noticed and were grateful for their care in arranging your visit.

Paragraph 3. In ending your bread-and-butter letter, of course you'll say thanks again for a wonderful visit. It's also nice to add that you hope to see your hosts again soon, or you'd like to have them visit you next time, or whatever is appropriate. Remember that in this kind of letter you're saying thank you not for a gift but for the chance to visit your friends or family. So it makes sense to say specifically that you enjoyed spending time with them.

Here's what Charlie Cool and Mary Sunshine wrote when they got home from their visits.

April 21, 19—

Dear Mr. and Mrs. Reilly,

Thank you very much for the great time at your house over spring vacation. It was terrific to get to spend a whole week with Kevin, and it's nice to know we're still best buddies even though he moved away.

I especially liked going to the auto racing museum in Watkins Glen. Those old cars are really amazing, and I never would have seen them if you hadn't taken us there.

Thanks again for a wonderful vacation. I hope Kevin can come and visit me next time.

Yours truly,
Charlie C.

—— ✤ ——

April 22, 19—

Dear Aunt Lily and Uncle Tom,

I had such a wonderful time visiting you over spring vacation — thank you so much! I'm still thinking about the trip by burro down into the Grand Canyon — it was the most exciting thing I've ever done! When my pictures come back, I'll send you copies if they turn out okay.

I feel pretty lucky to have you for relatives. You

did so many things to make my trip special, like going to the place where we could see silver jewelry being made. And it was great to spend time with Susie — she's awfully cute and I think she got to know her big cousin Mary pretty well.

Many thanks again for everything. I hope to see you again soon. Say hi to Susie for me.

Love,
Mary

Thank-Yous for Favors

The people who do special favors for you are likely to be adults. Perhaps a neighbor you've worked for has recommended you to her friend who wants her lawn mowed. Maybe the mother of one of your friends made time to drive the whole group of you to the skating rink every Saturday all year. What about your dad's friend who was able to get you the watch you've been saving up for at less than retail price? Or perhaps your mother's friend who works at the television station got you a pass to see one of the shows being made.

Favors like these don't usually cost the person who does them any money; nevertheless, they are valuable. And the person who did the favor had to go out of his or her way to do it. Such a person will be pleased to know that you were happy about it, and he or she will feel that your gratitude and appreciation made doing the favor worthwhile.

Like other thank-you notes, this kind can be fairly short. Start it the same way you started the others.

Paragraph 1. Say specifically what you're thanking the person for, and mention a detail or two that tells why you enjoyed or appreciated what he or she did. You might say:

> Thank you very much for recommending me as a
> baby-sitter to Mrs. Wright. She's hired me to sit
> for the twins two afternoons a week all year, and
> I'm thrilled!

Specific details that express your own feelings or observations make your thank-you note more personal; they make it clear that you really did have a good time or appreciate what the person did for you.

Paragraph 2. As in the other kinds of thank-you notes, this is a good place to say something nice about the person who did you the favor. You could say:

> You were really nice to remember that I was
> looking for baby-sitting work, and it was your
> kind words about me that got me this job.

Remarks like this may sound a little sugary-sweet to your ears, but remember, most people are happy to be told how nice and kind they are.

Paragraph 3. Again, repeat your thanks in slightly different words; that's all that's needed here. You can add a phrase like "I hope to see you soon" if it's appropriate, and then sign off politely.

Here are the thank-you notes Charlie Cool and Mary Sunshine wrote to people who did favors for them.

April 26, 19—

Dear Mr. Barnes,

I can't think of a good enough way to thank you for taking me and my dad to the Yankees' locker room before the game last Sunday. It was the greatest experience of my whole life. All my friends are totally jealous that I got to shake hands with the stars and that I got a signed baseball besides.

I know you had invited my dad to the game, and you were really nice to let me come along too. I hope you know how much it meant to me!

Thank you so much for an afternoon I'll never forget.

Yours truly,
Charlie Cool

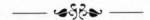

April 28, 19—

Dear Mrs. Kaufman,

Thank you a million times for including me yesterday in your behind-the-scenes visit to the zoo. When Lisa told me what we were going to do, I couldn't believe it. It was fascinating to see a real-life reporter at work, and it was absolutely fantastic to see all the baby animals in the zoo nursery. My favorites were the baby spider monkeys — they are darling!

I feel pretty lucky to have a best friend whose mom has such a neat job. And I think it was especially nice of you to invite me along with Lisa to the zoo.

Thank you again. I had a really fabulous time.

Sincerely yours,
Mary

Thank You for Being You

This kind of note might be called an "appreciation note." It's what you might write to a teacher, a camp counselor, a coach, a youth-group leader, or anyone you've spent a lot of time with who has been important to you in some way. In an appreciation note, you're not saying thanks for a specific gift or event; instead, you're telling the person how much you have valued his or her friendship, help, or support. You're really saying "thank you for being you."

Does this sound like a stupid kind of letter to write? It's not. You might be surprised to know how very much people love to get letters like this. It makes them feel that they have made a difference in your life and that you found your relationship with them valuable and important. And you might also be surprised to learn how few people take the time to write such letters.

An appreciation note can be very short (just one paragraph is usually fine). Try to use the same words you would say in speaking to the person. If it's too flowery, it will sound fake.

Begin your note by explaining why you're writing it. Then go on to mention something specific that has made this person special to you. If you just say he or she is "nice" or "wonderful" or "great," you could be talking about anybody. Instead, try to refer to something the person did or to something about his or her personality, like a great sense of humor or a calm and patient attitude. You may find you've got three or four sentences' worth of things like this to say.

End your note with another general statement of your

feelings about the person, and then you're finished. Don't be surprised if you get a note back that thanks you for your thank-you — people truly are happy to receive this kind of note.

Charlie Cool wrote an appreciation letter to his basketball coach.

April 30, 19—

Dear Mr. Hawkins,

I just wanted to tell you how much I enjoyed playing on your team this year. You taught me a lot about the game, and you made even the practices fun. When I messed up a play, you made me feel okay by making a joke instead of getting mad. Thanks for being a great coach. I hope I get to play on your team next year.

Yours truly,
Charlie C.

Remember, the important points about a thank-you note are:

· Write it soon.
· Include details to make it personal.
· Be sure to say "thanks."

4. Apologies ஃ

Of course you probably almost never do anything wrong, or dumb, or thoughtless, but sometimes even perfect kids make mistakes! It's hard to say "I'm sorry," because those words are an admission that you were wrong, and that's a very difficult admission to make.

Most people hate to feel that they've done something wrong. It makes them feel bad about themselves. So people often try to justify whatever it was they did, even though deep down they know it was wrong. Someone once said that the hardest words to say, and the most welcome ones to hear, are "I was wrong, and you were right."

But making an apology when it's called for is important. You may feel that if you don't do anything about a problem you've caused, it will eventually go away and be forgotten. Usually, however, the other person doesn't really forget. He or she might never mention the problem again, but the fact that you never apologized will color your relationship from then on.

For small problems, a quick apology in person is all that's needed. But for something more serious, a written note is often the best way to handle things, and the easiest as well. Does that sound absurd? Think back to the last time you told someone you were sorry about something you did. Did you really sound as if you meant it, or was your voice sullen and your facial expression angry? Apologizing is so difficult to do gracefully that your words often don't have the effect you wanted. And a grudging apology is only slightly better than none at all.

It's easier to admit you were wrong when you're not faced with the person you hurt. On the phone or in person, you may feel so embarrassed about whatever it is you're apologizing for that you can't even get the words out. You stumble over your sentences, and there are long empty pauses when you can't think of how to say what you mean. When you write a note, though, your embarrassment or the blow to your pride doesn't get in the way of your words; you can spend enough uninterrupted time to choose exactly what you want to say and how to say it.

Another thing that makes apologies difficult is that the other person may still be angry at you. A written apology gives that person a chance to read what you have to say without being able to interrupt with angry words and throw you off the track. He or she may even read your note more than once, each time with less anger and more willingness to accept your apology.

On the other hand, the person you're apologizing to may also be feeling pretty unhappy about the whole problem. Sometimes this makes a person jump into the conversation and say something like "Oh, that's okay, don't worry about it," before you've even gotten the apologetic words out of your mouth. But this kind of attempt to make you feel better and smooth things over doesn't work very well, because if you know you were in the wrong, you need to get your apology out there so the other person can accept it. By writing a letter, you can be sure the other person will read through your whole statement and will understand how sorry you feel.

Often a written apology seems more sincere than a verbal one. After all, if you took the time to write a letter, you must have really meant it when you said you were sorry. A letter makes it clear that you've thought the problem over, and that you want to set things right.

Finally, and this may be the most important reason of all, writing a letter of apology makes you feel better. There's something about sitting down and writing out your feelings and your hopes to improve the situation that lifts your spirits. You've gotten rid of that burden you were carrying — being mad at yourself for doing something mean or stupid, worrying that the problem will never get solved and you won't be able to look the person in the face again — and now you can put it all behind you. That feeling alone is worth writing a letter, isn't it?

When to Write an Apology

Who should you write apologies to? Perhaps you and your best friend had an argument that mushroomed into a major quarrel, with nasty words and hurt feelings on both sides. Be the first one to write an apologetic note; it will make you feel better and will certainly be a big step toward mending the friendship.

Another situation that deserves a written apology is when you've lost or damaged something that doesn't belong to you. Maybe you borrowed your friend's tennis racquet and it got broken, or you mislaid the jacket you borrowed to go to a picnic and now it's lost forever. As well as offering to pay for the lost or broken item, you need to tell your friend you're sorry for being careless with something that was probably important to him or her. One benefit of writing this kind of apology is that your friend may be more willing to lend you something the next time. If you don't even care enough to apologize, your friend would have to be pretty dumb to let you borrow anything again.

There may be times when you owe an apology to an older person, rather than a friend your own age. Writing a note instead of just mumbling a quick "Sorry" in person makes a good impression on adults. It shows that you are responsible and that you recognize adults are people too, with feelings that can be hurt and possessions they care about. When you ruin a neighbor's flower bed by playing tag in her yard, a note of apology that includes an offer to pay for new plants will make your neighbor a lot less upset.

It's also possible that you have disturbed a neighbor in some other way — by making so much noise outside her house that you woke the baby from its nap, by angling your desk lamp so it shines right into her bedroom window, or by carelessly letting your dog use her lawn as a toilet. In cases like this, there's nothing you can pay to have fixed. However, an apologetic note that says you'll try not to let it happen again will be a big help in restoring peace in the neighborhood.

There are other situations in which a letter of apology makes a lot of sense. Perhaps you were hired to do a job of some kind, and you messed up. You might have forgotten to pick up the mail for a couple of days while the people next door were on vacation, or maybe you did a rotten job of raking the leaves or shoveling the snow because you were in a hurry to go to a movie. This kind of problem calls for a letter that says you're sorry and includes an offer to do the job over again for free (if that's possible). Such a letter is good business — it may be the only way you'll keep this particular job.

And then there are family apologies. Did you forget to write a thank-you note to Aunt Emily, who has now let your mom know how rude you were not to say thanks for the sweater she sent? Don't let this kind of situation get bigger and more bitter — write an apology to Aunt Emily right away (and include your belated thanks in your note!).

Perhaps you woke up in the middle of the night feeling ashamed of the bratty and downright ugly way you acted to your mom and dad at dinner. It may seem silly to write a letter to people who live in the same house, but a loving note of apology for your behavior can make you as well as your parents feel a million times better. You don't have to mail it — just leave it where they'll be sure to find it.

In fact, a written apology can resolve many difficult and awkward situations and is often the most important step in restoring peace and good feelings.

What Should You Say?

In an apology, the first and most obvious thing to say is "I'm sorry." It might be "I'm sorry I hurt your feelings" or "I'm sorry I broke your window" or "I'm sorry I forgot your party," but whatever the problem, say "I'm sorry" first.

But after that, what? Partly it depends on whether you

feel you did something wrong or careless. If you did, say so in plain words.

Here's what Charlie Cool wrote as an apology to the owner of a crafts shop.

June 7, 19—

Dear Mr. Miller,

I'm really sorry that my friends and I knocked over your whole outdoor display of pine-cone decorations. We shouldn't have been fooling around right next to your display, and I know it was a stupid thing to do. All I can say is that we weren't using our heads, and we'll know better next time. I understand why you told us to leave, since we probably couldn't have helped you make it look right again. But I'd be happy to come and sweep the store or something to try and make up for the trouble we caused you. Anyway, I wish it hadn't happened and I'm sorry.

Yours truly,
Charlie Cool

Similarly, saying "I was wrong to exclude you from the group at lunch, and I can imagine how upset and angry you felt" does the job of taking responsibility for the problem. Perhaps you feel there were good reasons for what you did — you and the group were discussing a surprise party for your friend, and that's why she was left out, for example — but you could probably have had this discussion at another time. Whatever your reasons, the fact is that you hurt her feelings, and that's what you need to apologize for.

What if you weren't wrong, though? Maybe you promised to meet a friend after school and go to the pizza place for a slice, but you broke your arm in gym class and had no time to get word to your friend before you were rushed by ambulance to the hospital. That's a pretty extreme example, but it makes the point — you couldn't help breaking your date, but your friend was angry that you didn't show up as you'd promised. For this kind of thing, you can say you're sorry without taking on the total responsibility. You might write from the hospital and say, "I'm sorry you were upset," and then go on to explain what happened to prevent you from coming.

Notice that there's a difference between "I'm sorry I upset you" and "I'm sorry you were upset." In the first version, you're taking the blame. In the second, you're expressing your understanding that someone else was distressed or inconvenienced by your action, even though you couldn't help it and didn't do it on purpose. And showing that you understand the other person's feelings is the most important part of your letter.

Here's the apology letter Charlie Cool wrote to his friend Jim.

June 13, 19—

Dear Jim,

    I guess you're pretty mad at me — I tried to call you but your mom said you didn't want to talk to me. So I'm writing this letter. I know you must have been upset this afternoon when I didn't show up to go with you to the swim-team try-outs, because I know you didn't want to be doing it by yourself in front of a bunch of strangers. But really, I would have been there if I could.

I was at the mall out in Kent with my mom and when we were ready to leave, her car wouldn't start. We had to wait for the tow truck to come and it took forever. I tried to call you a couple of times, but your line was busy, and then I had to go and wait around with my mom by the car. I came over to your house as soon as we got back, but you'd gone someplace.

Listen, I'm really sorry you're upset — I guess I would be too. But believe me, I did try to get there. Hope you won't be mad anymore when you get this.

> Your friend (I hope),
> Charlie C.

What else should you say in a letter of apology? Certainly if you broke or lost something, you should offer to pay for it or even enclose payment with the letter. Similarly, if you forgot to do something or did it poorly, your letter should contain a commitment on your part to do it over again; mention a specific date if you can, so the other person will know that you mean it.

Here's the way Mary apologized to her sister Anna who was working at college for the summer.

> June 15, 19—

Dear Anna,

This is a hard letter to write, and I know you're going to be mad at me and I deserve it. You know that white sweater you said I could borrow since you weren't using it? I was at the pizza place with Ilene and I accidentally spilled tomato sauce on it, and it won't come out.

I'm truly sorry about it — I know you liked that sweater a lot. I'm going to look for another one to buy to replace it. I don't know what else to say except I'm sorry. I hope you'll forgive me for being so careless.

Love,
Mary

In most apology letters, and especially in those you write to a friend, it's important to let the other person know that you hope the problem will be solved so your friendship can be continued. It's also important to say that the friendship (or family relationship or whatever) is valuable to you and you don't want to lose it.

This is how Mary apologized to her friend Ilene.

June 20, 19—

Dear Ilene,

I'm terribly sorry for what I did. When Teresa invited me to go to the circus, it sounded like fun and I sort of forgot that you and I were going to have a sleepover. I know it was a rotten thing to do and I wish I hadn't gone with her.

Please forgive me for acting stupid. We've known each other since first grade and I'd hate to lose your friendship. It means a lot to me to be your friend and I count on you to listen to my problems and tell me when I'm wrong. I sure was this time and I apologize.

Your friend,
Mary

Words like this sometimes sound kind of soppy and you may feel embarrassed to write them down in a note. But saying these things makes the other person feel better, and that's the whole point of an apology.

5. Letters of Condolence ❧

According to the dictionary, "condolence" means "sympathy with another in sorrow." After a person dies, letters of condolence are sent to his or her family to express sadness and sympathy. These expressions of sympathy and support from friends and family are tremendously important to the person whose loved one has died.

Think about how you would feel if someone close to you — a parent, a brother or sister, a best friend — died. You'd be feeling lost and alone. Letters of sympathy would assure you that lots of people still loved and cared about you, even though an important part of your life was gone. That would make you feel a little less lonely. And receiving condolence notes would tell you that the person you loved so much was important to many others as well. You would know that your feelings of grief and loss were shared by many other people, and that might help you feel a little better.

Often condolence letters are read again and again; they can provide much comfort as the person tries to get used to life without the one who has died. Because these letters describe the wonderful qualities of the person who died, they can help the survivor look back with nostalgia and happy memories as grief becomes less all-consuming. Your condolence note is truly a gift you're sending someone at a very hard time in his or her life.

A condolence letter can be the most difficult kind of note to write. You feel awkward, knowing that the person you're writing to is deeply grieved. You don't know what to say, and you're afraid of saying something that will somehow make the person feel even worse. Such feelings may make you put off writing a condolence letter for days or weeks; then you feel even more awkward, writing about a person's death long after it happened.

Feelings like this are perfectly normal. Most people, adults as well as kids, have trouble writing letters of sympathy after a death. But it's important not to let such feelings stand in the way of writing a condolence letter. A phone call to express your sympathy isn't enough for this sad occasion, though of course you may want to call in addition to writing your note.

Since a condolence letter is such a personal expression of sympathy and support, it must be hand-written. And, though it's best to do it as soon as possible after you hear the sad news, it's never too late to write a note of sympathy. Perhaps you didn't hear about someone's death until months after it happened; perhaps you simply meant to write but couldn't find the right words. Whatever the reason, sit down and write the note right now. Don't worry that referring to a death long after it occurred will bring back unhappy feelings to the person you write to. He or she hasn't forgotten those feelings, and hasn't forgotten the person who died. Your note, late though it may be, will still bring comfort and welcome sympathy.

Who Should You Write To?

When a relative dies, you should write to his or her spouse and children. Write to Grandma if Grandpa dies, and also to your aunts and uncles who are their children. When someone in a friend's family dies, such as a grandparent, a note to your friend can be a great help.

Would it be silly, or in bad taste, to write a condolence letter when a pet dies? Not at all. Pets are often beloved members of a family, and their loss can cause a great deal of sadness. A note of sympathy to your friend whose cat was run over or to your aunt whose spaniel died of old age will be very much appreciated.

What do you do when someone you have known dies, but you don't know his or her family? It might be someone like your fourth-grade teacher whom you liked a lot but whose husband you've never met, or a person who worked with your mom or dad and whom you saw and chatted with lots of times at the office. You can find out the name and address of that person's spouse or children and write a short condolence letter. Even if you feel awkward writing to someone you have never met, do it anyway. Your note will mean a lot to the people who are grieving.

What Should You Say?

Letters of condolence need not be very long. It's usually best to keep your note short, saying only what you genuinely feel.

Paragraph 1. The first thing to say in any condolence note is that you were sorry to hear of the person's death.

There are various ways to phrase this statement. "I was very sorry to hear about your grandfather's death" and "Even though I knew she had been sick a long time, hearing the news of Grandma's death was just terrible" are both fine. You may want to mention how you found out; you might say, "My mom told me today that Great-Uncle Charlie had died, and I was awfully sorry to hear it," or "I was really sad when Mike Evans told me that Mr. Wilkes had died — we were both on the baseball team he coached three years ago."

If phrases like "passed away" or "departed" are generally used in your family or community, you'll probably want to use them in your note. But don't be afraid to use words like "death" or "died." They describe what has actually happened, and people are often grateful when others don't beat around the bush.

Paragraph 2. Here is where you can write down some of the reasons you'll miss the person who has died. Recall some of his or her special qualities; describe an experience the two of you shared; mention something special he or she did for you. This part need not be very long; just include one or two things that stand out in your memory. You might say:

> He had such a great sense of humor, and his warmth made everyone around him feel happy and special. I'll miss those silly snow fights he always organized, and his booming laugh when a snowball went down his neck. He was so much fun to be with!

You might think it's odd to write about your own experiences in a condolence note, but keep in mind that the person you're writing to doesn't necessarily know all about your relationship with the one who has died. Expressing your feelings about that person, and the experiences and memories that created those feelings, tells the survivor that there is a wide circle of friends and relatives who all have their own reasons to feel sad about the death. It's good for the survivors to have this evidence of how well loved the person was.

What if you didn't know the person who died very well? For instance, perhaps your friend's parents are divorced and you hardly knew her father who just died. You won't have many personal memories of your own to write about, but you can say you know your friend loved him a lot and recall things she's told you about him. Focus on your friend's feelings and express your sympathy for her sadness.

Paragraph 3. This is the end of your letter. It's a good idea to express your sorrow and sympathy again here, and to offer your help and support if that seems appropriate. Even if you can't think of any specific way you can help, the offer makes the person you're writing to feel less alone. If you wish to mention the consolation you or the person you're writing to can find in religious beliefs, this is a good place to do so. You might say:

> It's hard to find words to express my sadness and sympathy at the loss of Uncle Joe. I know he'll be missed by everyone who knew him. And I know God is looking after him now.

Or:

> It must be so terrible to have your mother die that I can't even imagine it. Please call me or come

over anytime. I'm here to give you any help I can, and I want you to know you're not all alone at this sad time.

For a family member or close friend, don't be shy about using words like "love"; ending your letter with "Much love, Bill" or "Lovingly, Karen" sends a message of caring and concern. For someone you don't know that well, a traditional closing for a condolence note is "With deepest sympathy"; it sounds formal, but it conveys your strong feelings of sorrow. Of course, you can use ordinary closings like "Sincerely" or "Yours truly" if you prefer.

Here is the condolence letter Mary Sunshine wrote to her grandmother after her grandfather died.

June 24, 19—

Dear Grandma,

I was so sad when I heard that Grandpa had died. Mom told me last night, and I haven't been able to think about anything else all day.

I think he was the best grandfather anyone ever had. He always seemed happy to see us when we visited you or when you came down here. And he was lots of fun to do things with. I remember when I was really little, he tried to teach me to skip stones on the lake, and he was so proud of me when I finally did it. Last year, I remember how much he laughed when we tried to sing him that weird song from camp, and then he taught us the words he knew to it when he was a kid.

I wish he hadn't died. I'm going to miss him an

awful lot, and I know you and everybody else in the family will miss him too. I'll see you very soon. Until then,

Much love,
Mary

Charlie wrote a condolence letter to his friend Kevin when Kevin's dog died.

June 26, 19—

Dear Kev,

What a shame about Daisy — it must be really tough for you.

It's kind of hard to believe she died — she was part of your family as long as I've known you. Last time I saw her, she seemed pretty quiet, but she was still wagging her tail and following anyone who went into the kitchen just like she always did. I remember that time she slept out in your backyard with us and got skunked — all three of us smelled for days.

I bet you're feeling lonely without her. Call me if you want to talk.

Your friend,
Charlie C.

Condolences to Someone You Don't Know Well

If you're writing a condolence note to a person you've never, or rarely, met, you should start it a little differently. It's important to identify yourself right away so the person reading the letter will know who sent it. You might say:

I was very sad to learn of Mrs. Morgan's death. You don't know me, but I was in her kindergarten class six years ago.

Then go on to explain why you felt strongly enough about the person who died to write this letter. Mention your memories of the person, or your feelings about him or her. You could say something like:

I thought I was lucky to be in Mrs. Morgan's class. I had been scared about starting school, but she was so kind and friendly, I couldn't stay scared.

End with another statement of your sorrow and sympathy; you can be a little more formal here if you feel it's more appropriate. You might say:

I'm sure lots of other kids who had her for a teacher will be as sad as I am to know that she died. Please accept my deepest sympathy in your loss.

Here are the condolence letters Charlie Cool and Mary Sunshine wrote to people they didn't know very well.

June 27, 19—

Dear Mrs. Barnes,

I wanted to tell you how sorry I was to hear that Mr. Barnes died suddenly. You don't know me, but my dad worked with Mr. Barnes and I met him a few times.

He was a really great person, and I'll never forget how kind he was to arrange for Dad and me to go into the Yankees' locker room and meet the players. He knew I'm a baseball nut and that was why he went out of his way to do that for me.

I'm very sad that this terrible thing happened to him. Please accept my sincere sympathy.

Yours truly,
Charlie Cool

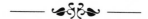

June 30, 19—
Dear Mr. and Mrs. Jones,

I was so upset to hear about your daughter's accident. You might not remember me, but I knew Cindy last year at camp. She and I were in the same cabin.

I can't believe she's dead. I was looking forward to seeing her again this summer. We had a lot of fun together last year — both of us hated archery and I don't think either of us ever hit the target, but we laughed about it a lot. She was a really nice person, and she was the only one in our cabin who learned to do the butterfly stroke the right way in swimming.

I'll miss her a lot this summer at camp, and I'm sure all her friends and her family will miss her very much. I just wanted to tell you how sorry I am that it happened.

Sincerely yours,
Mary Sunshine

Remember that the most important thing about a condolence note is sending it, no matter whether you think it's perfect or not. The exact words you use are less important than the fact that you send your written expression of sympathy and caring. So even though no one likes to think about death, write a condolence note as soon as possible. You may be surprised to learn how much it helps people who are grieving to know that you're thinking of them.

6. Congratulations ह▹

When you hear about something special that's happened to a friend or relative, a note of congratulations is a wonderful way to share that person's happiness. Many people don't take the time to write these short letters; they don't realize how great the person who gets them will feel.

What kinds of occasions are worth your written congratulations? First of all, there are all those major events in people's lives. Do you have an older sibling or a cousin who's graduating from either high school or college? A little note from you is a lot more personal than a card you buy. Is an older family member or friend, like your favorite baby-sitter when you were little, newly engaged or about to get married? He or she will be surprised and delighted to get your note of congratulations or best wishes. (By the way, it is traditional to offer wedding congratulations to the groom, not to the bride. To her you say "best wishes.")

If adult friends or relatives are celebrating a special wedding anniversary — their twenty-fifth or even their fiftieth — they'll be thrilled to hear from you on this happy occasion. Many adults, of course, write congratulations to the parents when a baby is born. And you can do this too, if you like.

What about awards and honors? Perhaps your cousin or a friend's older brother got a football scholarship to college or has been admitted to the Air Force Academy. Or maybe a girl you know has just been named valedictorian of her class. Why not send a brief note saying how happy you are for him or her? A few written words of congratulations are a great way to recognize that person's hard work and accomplishments.

If an article about your friend's or relative's achievement or an announcement of the wedding plans has appeared in the local newspaper, it's nice to cut it out and send it along with your letter. No one ever has enough copies of articles like this — in addition to putting one in a scrapbook, the person will probably send others to faraway relatives and friends. Be sure to write the date of the article and the name of the newspaper in the margin, or cut out that information from the top of the newspaper page and attach it to the article with tape. People like to know exactly when and where news about them was published.

What Should You Say?

It's fun to write letters of congratulations. There's good news to talk about and everyone is cheerful and proud. Feel free to be as enthusiastic as you like. While phrases like "you'll be the best running back State U has ever had" or "you're the best grandparents in the whole world" might not be strictly true, a little exaggeration is okay.

Your congratulatory letter can be very brief. The point is to let the person know you've heard the news and you're sharing his or her happiness.

Paragraph 1. Start out by telling what you're congratulating the person for. For instance, beginning with "I just heard that you and Bob are engaged" lets your cousin know why you're writing to her. And of course you want to say right away how happy or proud you feel. You might say:

> Your mom just called mine to say that you won first prize in the all-city violin competition. That's great!

Paragraph 2. This is the place where you talk about how hard your friend worked for this award or how terrific you think your relative is. You might say:

> I know you really worked hard. I used to see you coming back from your five-mile run every morning when I was getting up. You definitely deserve this track scholarship.

Or:

> I feel like part of your wedding plans since I'm the one who introduced you to Bill. I remember when you were baby-sitting and dropped me off at day camp where he was my counselor. I knew right away that you were meant for each other. And I was right!

Paragraph 3. At the end of your note you'll want to repeat your congratulations and add best wishes for the future. You might say:

> Congratulations again to the best grandparents in the world. I hope you have many more wonderful years together.

Or:

Again, best wishes. I'm sure the rest of your married life will be as much fun as your wedding was.

Here are the letters of congratulations Charlie Cool and Mary Sunshine wrote.

July 1, 19—

Dear Katie,

This is kind of late, but congratulations! It's great that your debating team won the championship. I just found out about it in the round-robin letter your brother Drew sent me.

I wasn't really surprised, though. I remember all those times when I was at your house and you were telling me and Drew all the reasons we couldn't do stuff. I guess it was good practice! Seriously, I always knew you were really smart, and now the whole city knows.

Congratulations again! I'm proud to be your cousin.

Bye for now,
Charlie C.

July 1, 19—

Dear Miss Ames,

My mom just showed me the announcement in the newspaper about your wedding plans, and I wanted to say how happy I am for you.

The picture in the paper was great, and I think

Frank Sullivan is so lucky to be marrying you (he certainly looks handsome). I hope you'll still be teaching art in our school next year.

 Best wishes for a very happy marriage.

Your friend,
Mary Sunshine

Whenever something special happens to people you know, a short note of congratulations is a great way to tell them you share in their pride and happiness.

7. Invitations and Replies ❧

If you're planning to have a party, of course you'll need to invite the guests. And there are lots of other kinds of social events that require invitations of some sort. Most often you'll be inviting people informally by phone. It would seem a little absurd to write to your friend down the street to invite him to come to your house for dinner or to go with your family to a baseball game.

For parties, though, invitations by mail are better. When the date, time, and place are written down on the invitation, everyone has that information and there's no chance that your guests will turn up on the wrong day.

In the old days, most invitations were written by hand or specially printed for people who were giving parties. This kind of invitation is still used for weddings and other formal occasions, such as bar mitzvahs. But now most people buy party invitations at the stationery store and fill in the blanks. You can choose funny or flowery or plain styles, and you can add any information you want. For instance, even if the invitations have spaces to write in only the date, time, and place of the party, you might want to add the reason you're giving it (such as your birthday or a surprise party for someone else).

Invitations often have a line that says "R.S.V.P." with a blank space after it for the host's phone number. The letters R.S.V.P. stand for the French phrase *Répondez s'il vous plaît*, which means "Please reply." When you receive an invitation, it's basic politeness to reply, whether or not a response is requested. After all, the host wants to know how many guests are coming to the party, and whether you received the invitation in the first place.

Often you can phone to say that you'll be there or that you're sorry but you're already busy that day. However, if you receive a formal invitation, such as one to a fancy wedding and reception, you are expected to mail your reply. A reply card to be filled out and returned is usually enclosed with the invitation. It's not likely that you'll be invited to a formal wedding that your parents aren't invited to, so your reply will usually be included on their reply card.

Sometimes, though, you might want to write a letter in addition to sending back the card. What if your family is invited to the wedding of your old baby-sitter, but it's the same date as your mom's birthday and your parents are having a big party? You might want to let your baby-sitter know that you're really sorry you can't be at her wedding and explain why. It's better to write than to try to call her, since she's probably so busy with wedding plans that she can barely get to the phone.

When a lot of information needs to be exchanged, both the invitation and the reply are likely to be letters, not cards or phone calls. For instance, if you invite a friend who lives in another town to visit you, there will be details to explain, and it's good to have it all written out for her to show to her parents. They need to know how to get to your house, they need to feel certain that your parents know about this plan and that it's okay with them, and they need information about what day and what time your friend should arrive.

It used to be considered improper for kids to invite their friends themselves; the polite thing was for one kid's parent to write to the other one's family to extend the invitation. And it's still a good idea for your mom to call your friend's mom to confirm the details after you've written to your friend.

Here's what Mary Sunshine wrote to her friend Bonnie, who lives in another town.

July 3, 19—

Dear Bonnie,

Guess what! I got a great idea and my mom says it's okay with her. Here it is — you're invited to come to my house the Sunday before camp starts and stay the whole week. Then my dad will drive both of us up there on the day camp starts.

My brother Mark will be away at Grandma's that week, so he won't be around to bother us. And there's a big fair in town we can go to on the weekend.

I sure hope you can come! Let me know right away. If your parents can't drive you here, you could take the bus (I'm sending a bus schedule so you can decide which one to take). My mom and I could pick you up at the bus station. Be sure to bring all your stuff for camp with you!

I can't wait to see you! My mom says to tell you she'll call your parents sometime next week.

Love,
Mary

And here's what Bonnie wrote back.

July 10, 19—

Dear Mary,

Yes, I can come! It works out perfectly, because we're all going to my cousin's wedding in Pismo Beach on Saturday, so my parents can drop me off at your house on Sunday on their way home. I probably won't get there until about six o'clock — hope that's okay.

Remember Jessica from camp last year? I found out she's going to be there again this summer — what a pain! But at least you and I will be in the same cabin.

I'm really looking forward to staying at your house. Thanks a lot for inviting me!

Love,
Bonnie

Here's what Charlie Cool wrote to his friend Kevin.

July 14, 19—

Hey, Kev —

Remember when we talked about getting together this summer? Well, my folks have rented a cottage on Lake Pearl for two weeks in August and they said I could invite you for the first week (my sister gets the other one). We're going up there on August 3 and it would be great if you could come the same day.

There's a train that gets into Poughkeepsie about three o'clock and we could pick you up there. Be sure to bring your fishing gear and your sleeping bag, because we might camp out a night or two. Do you still have that old two-man tent? If you do, bring it!

Sure hope you can come — it seems like a long time since I saw you and it would be great to get together. Your folks can call mine if they have any questions. Let me know soon!

Your buddy,
Charlie C.

And here's what Kevin wrote back.

July 21, 19—

Yo, Charlie —

Great to hear from ya! And I talked my folks into letting me come to Lake Pearl with you — sounds great! I'll be taking that train you mentioned that gets into Poughkeepsie at three on August 3, and I could take the noon train back the next Sunday.

I'll definitely bring the fishing stuff, but about the tent, didn't I tell you what happened? I left it in the garage without drying it out after a big rain and it got all moldy and my mom made me get rid of it. But my brother John has one and maybe he'll let me borrow it. We've gotta promise to take care of it, though.

Anyway, it'll be great to see you — thanks a lot for asking me.

Later,
Kev

Whenever you send a written invitation, be sure to include all the necessary information: what's going to happen, date, time, place, and how to respond. And when you receive an invitation yourself, write or call soon to give your reply.

II. Business Letters ❧

Business letters are usually addressed to people you don't know very well — people you've probably never even met. These letters have a specific purpose, rather than just saying hi to a friend. Many adults write business letters as part of their jobs, but kids too write business letters for various reasons. A business letter might be a request for information about the place you're going on vacation or the topic of a school report. If you've lost a part to a game or your cat ate the instructions, you can write a business letter to the company that makes the game to ask how to get a replacement. Or maybe you've been trying to find a particular item to buy for a friend's birthday gift, but none of the stores near you has it. Write a business letter to the manufacturer to find out if you can buy it by mail.

Another kind of business letter is a "compliment" letter. You might write a compliment letter to a company whose policies you approve of. For example, a grocery store chain that is giving customers a rebate for reusing grocery bags deserves a letter that expresses your appreciation of this environmentally friendly policy.

On the other hand, you may want to write a complaint

letter if a product you bought doesn't work or if it's not what the ads made you think it would be. You can also write to a television station to say you think a certain program is stupid or boring. Letters from viewers are taken seriously by the people at television stations when they plan their programming. A complaint letter is also a good way to express your dissatisfaction with a store whose employee treated you rudely or cheated you.

Other kinds of business letters include fan letters to stars, letters that express your opinion about issues that are important to you, and letters that are intended to be published in newspapers or magazines. You may even have ideas for improving various products that you want to write down and send to the manufacturer.

You might think it's strange for kids to write business letters, but it's not. After all, if you don't write to say what you think, companies and governments won't know how their actions are affecting people like you. You're a person who buys things, and someday you'll be a voter. Your opinions matter.

How Should It Look?

It's important to write all your letters clearly enough so people don't have trouble reading them, but it's especially important for business letters. The people who receive your business letter don't know you, and if your letter is illegible, they may not bother to try to figure out what it says.

If possible, type all your business letters so they are completely readable. Otherwise, write in dark blue or black pen and use your neatest handwriting. It's not a good idea to use curlicues and heart-shaped dots for your i's in business letters; be plain and businesslike. Write on one side of your paper only; people in offices aren't used to two-sided letters, and you want to make things easy for them.

If you can use a word processor, it will be simple to make changes in your letter until it's just right. If not, write a rough draft first; then go over it to make sure you've said exactly what you want to say clearly and briefly. Rewrite or type it for the final copy you will send. Whether you use a word processor or a pen, do read over your finished letter to check for spelling or grammatical mistakes. You want your letter to make a good impression on the person who reads it.

You might want to make a copy of your business letter before you mail it, or keep it filed on your computer disk. Most business people do this; it gives them an easy way to keep track of what they wrote and when they sent it. A copy that you keep will let you know how long it's been since you sent your letter, and it will help you figure out whether the reply answered the questions you asked.

Basics of a Business Letter

Business letters are written in a more formal style than personal letters. There used to be very strict rules about how to arrange all the parts of the letter — how many spaces or lines to leave between parts, formal phrases that had to be used, and so on. But today business letters don't all follow exactly the same style. Still, there are some basics that every business letter should contain.

RETURN ADDRESS

Unless you have stationery with your name and address already printed at the top, put your return address in the upper right corner of the page. You can leave off your name, since you'll put it at the bottom of the letter, but be sure to include your street address and your city, state, and ZIP code. If someone might call you on the phone in response to your letter, rather than writing back, add your telephone number (with area code) as the last line of the return address.

DATE

In a business letter, the date can go below the return address on the right (skip a line between them so the date doesn't look like part of the return address). Or you can put the date at the left margin, a line or two below the return address and above the inside address.

INSIDE ADDRESS

Obviously, the name and address of the person you're writing to go on the envelope, but in a business letter they are also included in the letter itself. You may think this is odd — after all, the letter got to the person whose name was on the envelope, so why does he or she need it again? But in an office, the envelope may be thrown away before the letter is even read, or the letter may be passed around to various members of the organization. It's important for all these people to know who originally received the letter, so they can refer to it correctly when they reply.

This address at the beginning of the letter is called the inside address. It goes a couple of lines below the date, at the left margin. The inside address consists of the name of the person you're writing to, his or her title (if you know it), the name of the company or organization, the street address, and the city-state-ZIP line.

If you don't know the name of a person to write to, don't worry. You can send a business letter to a company or an organization. It's a good idea, however, to give some indication of what department you'd like your letter to reach. For instance, a complaint letter to a business might be addressed to the Customer Service Department. Most companies have a department like this, and even if they call it something slightly different, your letter will get to the right place. If you haven't been able to find out the correct name of the department you want, make one up that sounds right to you.

SALUTATION

The salutation refers to the greeting line in your business letter. Always start with "Dear" and then use a courtesy title (Mr., Ms., Mrs., or Miss) followed by the person's last name — Dear Ms. Brown. For a man, it's almost always safe to use Mr. For a woman, unless you know she prefers to use Mrs. (married) or Miss (unmarried), it's best to use the more modern Ms. (If you can't tell whether the person is male or female, use the first and last names without a courtesy title — Dear Lee Jones.)

There are a few exceptions to this rule. If you know the person is a doctor, you should use Dr. before his or her last name. The same is true for other professional titles, such as Professor (Dear Prof. Green). For government officials and religious leaders, there are specific formal ways of address-ing a letter; you'll find this information on page 155.

If you don't know the name of a person to write to, you

can simply use the salutation "Dear Sir or Madam." Sometimes business letters start out with "To whom it may concern:" but this is a very cold and formal-sounding greeting.

The salutation in a business letter is followed by a colon. Skip a line before starting your letter.

CLOSING AND SIGNATURE

You won't want to end a business letter with "Love and kisses" or "Later, dude." Use something that sounds businesslike; good possibilities are "Sincerely," "Sincerely yours," and "Yours truly."

It's probably best to put the closing and signature in the same place as in a personal letter — at the lower right of your letter, lined up with the return address and date. Some business letters have the closing and signature at the left margin, lined up with the left edge of the letter itself, and you can do that if you prefer.

Skip a line or two under the closing and then add your signature — use both your first and last names. Underneath your signature, print or type your full name clearly. The reason for this is that many people have scrawly, illegible signatures, and without a printed or typed version to check, it's impossible to send a reply to the right person. If you're using a word processor or typewriter, leave three or four lines between the closing and your typed name so you'll have room to write your signature.

MARGINS

Like personal letters, business letters are easier to read if they have blank space at the top and bottom and at both sides. The side margins should be at least one inch. Keep the left margin nice and straight, but don't worry if the

BUSINESS LETTER

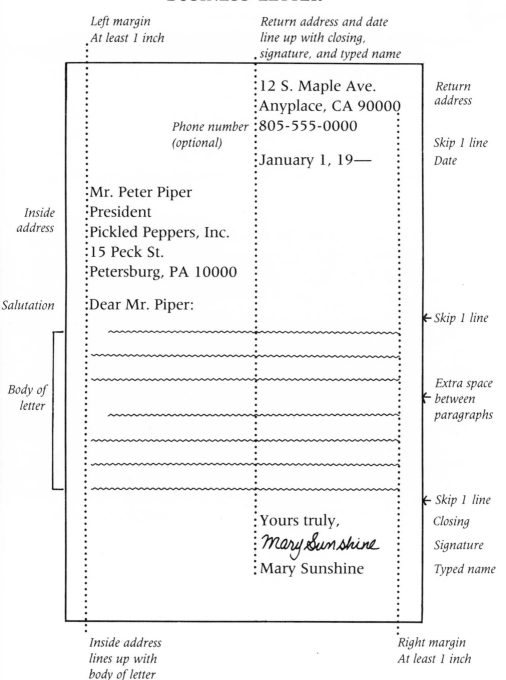

Left margin
At least 1 inch

Return address and date
line up with closing,
signature, and typed name

12 S. Maple Ave.
Anyplace, CA 90000
805-555-0000

January 1, 19—

Return address

Skip 1 line
Date

Phone number
(optional)

Mr. Peter Piper
President
Pickled Peppers, Inc.
15 Peck St.
Petersburg, PA 10000

Inside address

Dear Mr. Piper:

Salutation

← Skip 1 line

Body of letter

Extra space
← between
paragraphs

← Skip 1 line

Yours truly,

Mary Sunshine

Mary Sunshine

Closing

Signature

Typed name

Inside address
lines up with
body of letter

Right margin
At least 1 inch

right margin goes in and out a bit. It's better to put a long word down on the next line than to have it dangle sloppily into your right margin.

Letters look best when they are more or less centered between the top and bottom of the page. This means that if you are writing a very short business letter, you'll want to start your return address two or even three inches from the top edge. You can leave a little extra space between the parts of a short letter, so it doesn't look crammed into the top half of the paper. If your letter is quite long, though, start it closer to the top of the paper so it will all fit on one sheet. It's best to keep your business letters short enough to fit on one page; this makes them more likely to be read by busy people.

If you do have more than one page, don't forget to number every page after the first one.

PARAGRAPHS

Business letters are typed single-spaced, but it's a good idea to skip a line between the paragraphs. Otherwise your letter will look scrunched up and it will be harder to read.

Stationery and Envelopes

When you take the time to write a business letter, you want it to be treated seriously. Don't use your fancy pink stationery with the border of roses or your goofy notecards with cartoon cats all over them. Not only is personal stationery unbusinesslike, it's usually smaller than business stationery and it will get lost in an office's file drawer.

The best choice for business letters is plain white 8½" × 11" paper; regular typing paper, computer paper, or photocopying paper is perfect. Don't use dark-colored paper; it's harder to read than plain white, and it also doesn't photocopy well.

If you are writing your business letter by hand, it's okay to use lined white paper in the same $8\frac{1}{2}'' \times 11''$ size. Even three-hole notebook paper will be okay, though the holes can get caught or ripped as the letter is handled or filed.

Choose plain white envelopes, too, unless you have some that are already printed with your return address. Standard size is best, but you can also use the Commercial size (see page 16). Before you fold your letter to go into the envelope, be sure you've signed it!

Address the envelope the same way you address one for a personal letter (see page 11). Include your name in the return address in the upper left corner, and repeat the inside address from the letter on the envelope. Don't forget to put a stamp in the envelope's upper right corner before you mail it.

Finding Out Where to Send a Business Letter

Before you can send a business letter, you need to find out where it's going. Discovering the address of a company or a government office may require some detective work, but this kind of work can be a lot of fun. Here are some hints to help you get started on your search.

The easiest addresses to find are the ones in your own hometown. If you're writing to a local company, museum, college, or other business or institution, look in the white pages of your phone book.

Government listings (city, county, state, and federal) often appear in a special section of the phone book; look for it in the table of contents. Listings for state and federal government departments give the phone number of the nearest local office. If you're not sure which department handles the question you want to ask, make your best guess and then call. You might have to try a couple of different agencies or departments before you find the right one, but don't give up. Once you've found the department you want, ask for the name of the person to write to as well as the address, including the ZIP code.

Suppose you've decided to write to someone about a problem in your local public park. In the pages that list city government offices, you find nothing under "Parks Department." But you spot an entry for "Recreation and Parks Department," and under that there are entries for "Administration" and for "Parks Division" with phone numbers but no addresses. You could call either of these numbers and ask for help; explain what you plan to write a letter about and find out who to send it to at what address.

What if the business you want to write to is not located in your town? More detective work is called for. You have several possible ways to find the address you need. First, look on the packaging or information leaflet or any other paper you have; if a partial address is given, such as a city and state, that will give you a clue.

Many large companies, charitable or nonprofit groups, and even some government offices have 800 numbers — phone numbers with the 800 area code. Calls to 800 numbers are free, so this is a good way to start. You can call 1-800-555-1212 for 800 Directory Assistance; ask the operator if there is an 800 number listed for the organization or company you want to reach. You won't be able to get a street address from the operator, but you can call the 800 number of the company and get the address that way. Don't forget to ask for the name and title of a person to write to.

If no 800 number is listed for the organization you want, and if you know what city it's in, you can call Directory Assistance for that city (dial 1-area code-555-1212). Remember, though, that a fee is charged for every long-distance Directory Assistance call; in addition, once you have the phone number, you'll have to make another long-distance call to get the name and address to write to. So make sure it's okay before you start dialing all over the country — it may be easier and less expensive to go to the public library.

At the library you can find large reference books that list organizations of all kinds — corporations, associations, charities, just about anything you can think of. Ask the reference librarian to help you decide which of these directories might contain the address you want. Some libraries have telephone books for other cities and states, and of course these list addresses as well as phone numbers; try looking in one of these if you know what city you need.

Another way to track down addresses, especially for charitable organizations or nonprofit groups, is through their newsletters. Most groups send some kind of newsletter to their members from time to time, and the address of the group's main office will appear somewhere in its pages. Perhaps someone you know is a member of the group you want to write to and will give you a newsletter; or you might ask at your public library if there is any material from that group. (You may decide you want to become a member of the group yourself; when you write, ask if there is a special membership rate for young people or students.)

Usually, if you keep trying, you'll be able to find the address you need. And you may discover a whole world of amazing information while you search.

How to Write Your Business Letter

The point of writing a business letter is to make something happen. What do you want to happen as a result of your letter? And what do you want to say? Think these things through before you write your letter. Then write it as clearly, and as briefly, as you can. Give all the facts that are needed, but don't ramble on with unnecessary detail. When you're describing an event or problem, don't exaggerate; stick to the exact truth about what happened, and be realistic about what you expect to happen as a result of this letter. It's tempting to embroider a bit and make a problem sound worse than it was, especially if you're upset. But your letter will command more respect, and you're more likely to get what you want, if you explain things exactly as they occurred.

When you ask for free information, be as specific as you can. For instance, if you need facts and figures about Colorado for a school report due in March, say so in your letter; otherwise you may receive lots of beautiful photographs of tourist attractions, and no solid information, in April.

Finally, be polite. Whether you're asking for help or complaining about being treated rudely, your letter will have more impact if it's written in calm and polite language. The more reasonable you sound, the better results you'll get.

It's fun to keep a file of the business letters you write and the answers you receive. When you look through them later on, you may notice that some of your letters had more effect than others; can you figure out what you said or how you said it to make this happen?

It's also interesting to see which companies and organizations had the most helpful responses. When people decide which products to buy and which charities to give money to, they often don't have enough information to make the best choice. Your file of business letters will give you a lot of insight into how various companies and organizations deal with the public, and this will be a way to start making your own choices.

8. Complaints ॐ

Why should you bother to write a letter of complaint? Isn't it better just to forget whatever the problem is and get on with your life?

Of course, some minor annoyances aren't worth writing a letter about. But if you're really upset, you should write and complain. If you don't, the problem has no chance of being solved.

Before you start to write, think through your complaint. Jot down any factual information you have so you won't forget these details as you write. If you have concrete evidence of your problem, such as a receipt for something you bought, have it handy so you can refer to the exact amount of money and the date of the purchase in your letter. And decide what you want someone to do as a result of your complaint.

Considering these things ahead of time will help you write a letter that is short and to the point. Be as courteous as you can, but state your problem clearly and firmly. This might be the only opportunity you'll have to present your side of the story and get the problem solved.

Remember, though, that you may not get any answer at

all to your complaint letter. If you feel strongly about it, be sure to keep a copy of your letter; then, if you get no answer in a month or so, you can send a copy of that letter along with an explanation to the boss of that company, to the Better Business Bureau, to a newspaper consumer complaint column, or to a government agency that regulates that kind of business. However, you may decide that just writing your original letter was enough; putting your anger into words on paper probably made you feel better, even if it did nothing else! Most reputable companies do respond to complaint letters. If your letter doesn't get a reply, that tells you something about the company's attitude toward the public.

What Should You Say?

Paragraph 1. The beginning of your letter should tell the reader very briefly what your problem is and how you would like it solved. Be reasonable in what you expect; if a sales clerk was rude to you, you certainly deserve an apology from the company, but you won't get a check for a million dollars.

What if someone sent you a miniature robot as a present and when you opened the box, one of its arms was missing? You might write:

> I was given a robot (MiniRob, model # 12345) that was purchased at your store, and it is missing a part. I would like you to send me a new robot to replace it.

This explains very clearly what's wrong and what you want done about it.

Paragraph 2. In this part of your letter, you should

give any details that are important in explaining your complaint. Again, keep it as short as you can. In the letter about the robot, you might say:

> The robot was a gift from my aunt, so I don't have a receipt. But it came in a box with your store's name on it, and the enclosure card was also from your store.

Paragraph 3. End your letter by stating again what you expect to be done about the problem. If you can add any nice words about the store or whatever organization you're writing to, do so — it makes people feel more eager to do what they can to help. About the robot, you might say:

> I expect to receive a new robot that works from you soon. I know my aunt has always enjoyed shopping in your store, and I'm sure you'll solve this problem quickly.

Here are some complaint letters that Mary Sunshine and Charlie Cool wrote.

2 W. Main St.
Somewhere, NY 10000
914-555-0000

August 24, 19—

Customer Service Dept.
Cow and Spoon Clothing Co.
8 Little Dog Lane
Fiddle, CO 80000

Dear Sir or Madam:

I bought a dark-green turtleneck at your store when I was on vacation in the Rockies, and after only two washings the color has streaked and faded. I would like a replacement.

Both times the shirt was washed, I used warm water as the label says. After the first time I noticed some weird streaks on the sleeves. After the second time the whole shirt had light green streaks all over. The shirt is a Mountain Man, size medium, dark green.

I really like this shirt, so I hope you'll be able to send me another one soon. Your store is really great — could you send me a catalog or flyer along with the shirt?

> Yours truly,
> Charlie Cool

——— ✥ ———

> 12 S. Maple Ave.
> Anyplace, CA 90000
> 805-555-0000
> September 13, 19—

Mr. Jack Horner
President
KPIE-TV
1333 Plum St.
Anyplace, CA 90000

Dear Mr. Horner:

I watched the first episode of the new show *What a Good Boy Am I!* last night, and I thought the comments about girls were extremely nasty. I think you should take this show off the air.

I don't usually get upset about TV comedies, but this show is pretty hard for girls to watch.

Through the whole show, the main character Peter Pumpkineater makes fun of his sister, talks back to his mom, and plays nasty tricks on the girl next door. The other male characters think he's really funny. Meanwhile, the girls and women just cry; they never get mad and they never get to do the same things to Peter.

If you haven't watched this show yourself, I think you should. A lot of people in your audience are female, and I bet most of them hate this show as much as I do. I enjoy a lot of the other shows on KPIE, but this one made me change the channel. Please take it off your station.

Sincerely yours,
Mary Sunshine

——— ✥ ———

2 W. Main St.
Somewhere, NY 10000
914-555-0000

September 25, 19—

Miss Little Muffett
Customer Relations Dept.
Curds & Whey Department Store
149 Spider St.
Somewhere, NY 10000

Dear Miss Muffett:

I was in your store last Saturday, and one of your salesclerks, Mary Contrary, was extremely rude to me. I think Curds & Whey owes me an apology.

I went to the store to buy some bath oil for my

mother's birthday. When I found the right counter, I waited quite a long time for someone to help me. There were no other customers at the counter, but the three salesclerks were chatting near the cash register. I finally went over to them and said I wanted to buy some Tuffett Bath Oil. Two of them walked away, and the other, whose name badge said Mary Contrary, told me she was busy and I'd have to wait. But she wasn't busy — I could see that she just walked to the other side of the counter and started straightening a pile of little boxes. I went around there and asked her again to help me, and she said, "Oh, all right, what do you want?" in a very nasty way. I did buy the bath oil because that's what my mom wanted for her birthday, but I sure didn't enjoy being in your store.

I know I'm not the regular type of customer at a cosmetics counter — I'm a kid. But I had the money to pay for what I wanted, and I was polite. I feel I was treated very badly, and it makes me not want to go into Curds & Whey again. I hope you'll tell Miss Contrary that kids are customers too and should be treated as nicely as anyone else.

> Yours truly,
> Charlie Cool

Remember, the only way stores and organizations know that there is a problem is if you tell them. The better your letter is (clear, to the point, concise), the more likely it is that you'll get the response you want.

9. Fan Letters and Complimentary Letters ❧

Everyone likes to receive compliments, and famous people are no exception. If you want to compliment a performer, athlete, author, or other person in the public eye such as a politician, you can write a fan letter. Usually you've never met these people in person; you probably know them only through their performances in some field. But even though they don't know you personally, they want to hear from you. Fan letters tell performers that the audience likes what they're doing. And while really famous stars like to get fan letters, the less well-known actress or the athlete who's just starting his career may appreciate your letter even more.

To say something nice about someone who isn't famous, you can write a complimentary letter. Perhaps a salesclerk in a store was especially helpful and pleasant to you. Or maybe a bus driver took extra time to help you get where you wanted to go. Is there a waitress at your local coffee shop who always seems happy to see you and your friends when you go in for a hamburger on Saturday? You probably show her your appreciation by leaving a good tip each time, but you might also write a letter to her or to her boss to say what a good job she does.

Compliments on a job well done make people feel great. An expression of appreciation lets them know that someone notices and is grateful for their hard work and their efforts to be pleasant to customers. If you send your complimentary letter to the person's boss or the head of the company, it will be probably be passed on to the person you're writing about; meanwhile, your letter will let the boss know what a valuable employee he or she has.

You might wonder why a fan letter or complimentary letter should be a business letter instead of a personal one. Of course, one reason is that you're not a friend of the person you're writing to. But another, possibly more important, reason is that your letter probably will be read by several different people. A movie star's secretary may be the one to type and mail a reply; the waitress's boss will put your letter in her file. A business letter is easier for everyone to deal with.

Where to Send Your Letter

You may need to search a while to find an address for your fan letter or compliments, the same way you do for other business letters. You probably don't know the home address of your favorite rock star or baseball player, and you're not likely to find it listed in the telephone book. But here are some ideas for places to look.

You can always send a fan letter to the company or organization the person works for. For instance, mail your fan letter to a football player to his team's office. It will be forwarded to him.

For a television performer, the first place to try is your local station that aired the show. Look it up in the phone book and call the office; explain that you want to send a fan letter to a particular actor or actress, and ask for the address to send it to. The station is likely to have this information available. Another possibility is simply to send your fan letter in care of the TV station or the network.

For a movie star, a good place to send fan mail is the studio that made the person's most recent film. That company's name is always listed in the credits at the beginning and end of the movie and in newspaper ads for it.

What about rock stars? Take a look at the latest tape or CD the singer made; the name of the company that produced it will be shown on the packaging. There may even be an address listed on the box; look for the copyright symbol © and see if an address for the copyright owner is under it. If so, you're in luck; send your letter to the performer in care of that company, and it will be forwarded.

How else can you find a street address for a recording company, a sports team, or a movie or television studio? At the public library, you can look up the address in one of the directories that list companies and businesses; ask for help at the reference desk. For entertainers, look in the reference book called *Who's Who in Entertainment*, which lists performers and their office addresses. For sports players, a reference book titled *Sports Market Place* gives addresses of professional teams. For politicians, look in *Who's Who in American Politics* to find their office or home addresses.

To write to your favorite author, all you need to do is look in the front of one of his or her latest books. On the page where the copyright notice appears, you'll find the name of the publishing company and usually its address. You can also find the addresses of publishing companies in reference books like *Literary Market Place* at the library. Write to your author in care of the publishing company; he or she will love to hear from you.

When you send a fan letter in care of a company, make sure to address it clearly so that the mailroom people there will know it should be forwarded. Use "c/o" to indicate "in care of." Write the address like this:

Ms. Lucy Locket
c/o Lost Pocket Studio, Inc.
456 Pocket Lane
Bigtown, CA 90000

When you want to send a complimentary letter, you'll have to look up the address of the business where the person works. First try your local phone book. Even if it's a national company, it may have a local office that you can call to ask for the address of the main office. If it's not listed there, try the 800 information operator to see if the company has an 800 number you can call. Or you can ask at the reference desk in the public library for help in finding the address.

If the person you want to compliment works for a large company, you can send your letter either to the company's president or to the head of the personnel department. It's all right if you don't know his or her name; just address the letter to "President, XYZ Company" or "Director of Personnel, XYZ Company" and it will reach the right person.

Of course, if you're writing a letter about someone who works in a small business in your town, you can call and ask for the name of the owner; you can ask for the store's ZIP code, too. Then send your letter to the owner at the store's address.

What Should You Say?

Writing fan letters is fun; it puts you in touch with people you admire. But what exactly should you say? Start out by telling what it is you like about the person. What if you just finished reading an author's newest book and you thought it was really exciting? Tell her what you enjoyed about that book as well as any others she wrote that you've read. Maybe you've been a big fan of one rock star's music for a couple of years and now you think his latest release is the best he's ever done. Write him a letter and tell him so. Do you think a certain pitcher is destined for the Hall of Fame, and do you also think he seems really nice when he's interviewed on television? He'll appreciate hearing both of these things from you.

Major sports and performing stars usually have publicity photos available to send to fans. And most television and movie actors and actresses do too. But other people probably don't. Still, they'll usually send a letter thanking you for your fan letter. Of course you can ask for a photo or any other publicity material that might be available; people will send you whatever they can. Authors may have flyers about their books or their backgrounds; politicians might send you their latest report to the voters.

It's nice to say a little bit about yourself in a fan letter. In addition to giving your age and what grade you're in, you might want to tell what interests you have in common with the person you're writing to. For instance, an author will be interested to know that you like to write stories yourself or to hear about the kinds of books you like to read. If you love to play basketball, why not say so in the letter to your basketball hero?

Most people reply to fan mail. But sometimes it takes a really long time. Don't forget that your letter has to be forwarded, and that may take a while. In addition, the person you're writing to may be out of town on tour or just finishing her latest book or simply too busy to write back right away. So if you're writing your fan letter in connection with a class project, do it as early as possible.

Complimentary letters need a few more details than fan letters do. Of course the first thing you want to say is why you're writing. Tell the boss or personnel director what this person did that made you want to write this letter. Then give some details about where and when you encountered this person — on the Number 6 bus route last Tuesday afternoon or in the store's CD-and-tape department at your local shopping mall during the sale. Explain also who you are and what happened that was so special. How was that bus driver or salesperson helpful to you? The more specific details you give, the more effective your letter will be. Don't forget to give your age and your grade in school if that's not already part of your story.

Here is the fan letter Charlie Cool wrote to his favorite baseball player.

---

2 W. Main St.
Somewhere, NY 10000
October 1, 19—

Mr. Jack Benimble
c/o The New York Candleflames
789 Quick St.
New York, NY 10000

Dear Mr. Benimble:

I'm so happy you were traded to the Candle-flames! I've been a fan of yours ever since you started in baseball, and now I'll have a chance to see you play in person. Your last game against Detroit was fantastic, and that throw you made to Georgie Porgie for the final out was unbeliev-able. I play third base, too, on our school's Mod-ified team, and I hope someday I'll be as good as you are.

If you have a picture of yourself in the Candle-flames uniform, I'd really love to have one. And I'll be looking forward to seeing you at Jumpover Stadium next season.

Yours truly,
Charlie Cool

Here is a complimentary letter Mary Sunshine wrote after a trip to Seattle to see her grandmother.

---

12 S. Maple Ave.
Anyplace, CA 90000
October 17, 19—

Director of Personnel
Flybynight Airlines
101 Airport Rd.
Planeville, OR 90000

Dear Sir or Madam:

I'd like you to know what a great job your flight attendant Jill Jack does. I flew from Anyplace, CA, to Seattle, WA, on October 11 (flight #234), and Ms. Jack made it a very pleasant flight for me.

I'm a student at Anyplace Middle School and I was flying by myself for the first time. Ms. Jack asked me several times if I was okay and if I needed anything, but she did it without making me feel like a baby. She even found a teen magazine for me to read.

Ms. Jack was nice to the other passengers too. There was an older lady two rows ahead of me who had trouble getting on and off the plane. When she needed to go to the bathroom, Ms. Jack helped her up and made sure she didn't fall as she walked through the aisle. She was cheerful and she smiled a lot, so it didn't seem as if helping the lady was too much trouble for her.

When I got to Seattle, Ms. Jack made sure I found the person who was meeting me, even though I think she was off duty by then. She is a really nice person, and I wish she had been on my flight home. Flybynight Airlines is lucky to have her.

> Sincerely yours,
> Mary Sunshine

The whole reason for writing a fan letter or a complimentary letter is that you're happy and you want to praise someone. These letters are a lot of fun to write, and they mean a great deal to the people who receive them. So don't stop at thanking someone for a job well done — write a letter about it!

10. Requests 🕊

Lots of business letters you write are likely to be requests for information about a place or a topic; you may receive things like pamphlets, maps, or catalogs in reply. In other letters you might ask for information about a specific problem. For example, suppose you have lost the nylon cover for your bike helmet, and the store where you bought the helmet doesn't carry that brand anymore. You could write to the helmet manufacturer to ask where and how to get a new cover.

When you have to do a report for school, a good way to get up-to-date information is to write away for it. For a report on a certain place, try writing to the state's tourist agency (often located in that state's capital city), a city's chamber of commerce, or a country's tourism office or consulate (many of these are in New York City or Los Angeles; embassies are in Washington, DC). Ask the reference librarian for help in finding the addresses you need.

What if your report is about dairy farming? You could write to the U.S. Department of Agriculture in Washington, DC, to see if they will send you free information on this topic. Or you could check at the reference desk of the public library to see if there is an association of dairy farmers you could write to.

There are a huge number of associations of all different kinds. Most professions, such as medicine and banking, have at least one association that has a large membership. Anyone who is interested in gemstones or in chess may belong to an association of people with similar interests. People who suffer from a particular disease often belong to an association whose purpose is to help cure the disease. Bicycle enthusiasts may belong to cycling organizations that sponsor bike tours. Vegetarians, environmentalists, jewelry makers — there's probably no interest, hobby, or type of work that doesn't have an organization or association connected with it. And most associations have free information that they're happy to send to anyone who wants it.

How can you find these associations? Ask at the library. There is a three-volume reference set called *Encyclopedia of Associations* that lists just about any topic you can think of that might have a group of people who are devoted to it. Ask the librarian to show you how to use the books.

What if your family is planning a vacation in northern Virginia and you're crazy about exploring caves? You can write to the Virginia state tourist agency for information on places to see. But why not also write to an association of speleologists (people who explore caves) to see if they have information about caves in that area you can go into?

Suppose there is a hobby you'd like to find out about. Do you want to get serious about stamp collecting? Write to a philatelic (stamp collecting) association and ask for information for beginners. Do you love playing Scrabble? Maybe there's a group that matches up people who want to play Scrabble by mail. People who love dogs often belong to associations of owners of specific breeds or to groups that specialize in training and showing dogs. And if computers are your thing, you'll discover a whole world of computer associations and clubs.

There are other kinds of requests you may want to make by mail. Some companies, for example, have free stuff to send to people who ask for it. Many publishers will send you bookmarks and postcards advertising their books, and possibly even posters. Most large companies of any kind will send you free information about their products and services.

What about catalogs? Companies that sell their products by mail are happy to send you a catalog of the things you can buy from them. Publishers too have catalogs to send out; these tell about the new books they are publishing. Most catalogs are free, but some of them cost money — be sure to say in your letter that you only want the free kind.

If you're interested in how companies operate in the business world, you could write to a few and ask for copies of their annual reports. Companies that are listed on the stock exchanges in newspapers publish these fancy booklets every year. A company's annual report tells about what the company has done during the past year, what its profits and losses were, and what its plans are for the future.

The U.S. government publishes many booklets of information on all kinds of subjects. You can send for a catalog of these booklets: write to Consumer Information Center, PO Box 100, Pueblo, CO 81002, and ask for the Consumer Information Catalog. The booklets are all free or low-cost publications, and the catalog will tell you how to order any you decide you want.

You can get lots of other useful information from the federal government. Look in the government pages of your phone book for the Federal Information Center; this should be listed with an 800 number. If you can't find it, try calling 800 Information (1-800-555-1212) to get the number. The person you speak with at the Federal Information Center can give you addresses to write to for state information or facts about federal government departments of all kinds.

The United Nations is another good source of free information about the U.N. itself and about programs and holidays it sponsors. For example, if you'd like to know about U.N. projects to feed hungry people or save the environment, you can write a request letter for information to United Nations, United Nations Plaza, New York, NY 10017. It may take your letter a while to reach the right person, but eventually you should get lots of information back by mail.

What Should You Write?

A request letter should be very short. Generally you don't have to explain why you want whatever it is you're asking for. If it's available, it will be sent to you; if not, it won't.

It's important, however, to be as clear and specific as you can about what you are requesting. This makes it easier for people to fulfill your request.

If you need the information by a certain date, say so in your letter and be sure to send your request as early as you can.

Here is the request Charlie Cool wrote for information about a trip he and his friend Kevin were planning.

2 W. Main St.

Somewhere, NY 10000

November 5, 19—

Vermont State Tourist Agency
567 Mother Goose St.
Nowhere, VT 00000

Dear Sir or Madam:

I would like information about horseback camping tours in Vermont. A friend and I plan to vacation in Vermont next summer, and we would like to go on a trip for two or three days. We are students in middle school, and neither of us is a very experienced rider. But we have done a lot of camping out.

Can you please send me whatever information you have on groups that run this kind of trip? I especially need to know the dates the trips are scheduled for and how much they cost.

Please also send me a map of Vermont and information about other outdoor activities in the summer in southern Vermont.

Thank you very much.

Yours truly,

Charlie Cool

Here is the request Mary Sunshine sent to a store near Seattle.

12 S. Maple Ave.

Anyplace, CA 90000

November 8, 19—

Humpty Dumpty's Corner

890 Wall St.

King's Horses, WA 90000

Dear Sir or Madam:

I visited your store last month and bought a ceramic pendant on a silver-colored chain. I really love it and I would like to buy another similar one as a gift for a friend. Mine has a leaf design; I'd like to know what other designs are available and how much they cost. Could you please send me a catalog or a list of what is available? Thank you.

Sincerely yours,

Mary Sunshine

Request letters are an easy way to gather all kinds of information. Whatever you need to know, there's probably a way to find it through the mail.

11. Ideas for Improvements ⪼

Sometimes when you're watching TV or using an everyday product or eating in a fast food restaurant, you suddenly think of some way things could be improved. Maybe you've seen a TV commercial for a product that you really like, and you think the commercial isn't even mentioning the product's best features. You've got an idea for changing the commercial in a way that would make more sense to buyers.

Maybe you have a bike bag that is really terrific — it's just the right size for your stuff and it's got a neat design. But it attaches to the bike with buckles, and so it takes you forever to get it off the bike. You think the bag would be perfect if it had Velcro fasteners instead of buckles.

If you're trying to change your eating habits, and the only healthy item served at your favorite restaurant is green salad, you might wish that some vegetarian snacks, like celery sticks stuffed with peanut butter or mini-sandwiches of sliced apple and cheese, could be added to the menu.

Whenever you have a great idea for how something

could be improved, it's time to write a letter — unless you have thought up something totally new, not just a way to make an existing item better. If you have invented a board game, for example, talk with your parents about whether it's new and different enough to be sold. If they think it's really original and it might be something people would buy, it's best to talk to a lawyer. After all, you shouldn't give away a great idea for free. But for a minor improvement to something that already exists, go ahead and write.

Where Should You Write?

Many products have an address listed somewhere on the box or packaging. If not, look for the address in the reference section of the public library or call the company's 800 number and ask for it (see page 94).

You can send your letter to the president of the company. If you can find out his or her name, so much the better. If you can't, it's okay to address your envelope to "President, XYZ Company." Your letter will eventually get passed to someone else; but maybe the president will think your idea is so terrific, the company will start changing things right away. In a large corporation, there is probably a department where new ideas are dreamed up and tested, so you could write to the "Director of Product Development."

What Should You Say?

Since you're writing to suggest a wonderful idea, you'll want to give it the best possible presentation. Think your idea through as well as you can before you write your letter. Jot down some notes so you'll remember all the things you intend to say.

First, make it clear that you basically like the product and enjoy using it. This puts the person reading your letter in a cheerful mood, and he or she is more likely to think seriously about your idea. Then say briefly that you have an idea for improving the product.

Next, explain what it is that you don't like about the product the way it is now. Be very specific; this is your chance to pass on little anecdotes about the frustration you experienced when you ripped the package trying to open it or your puzzlement about why the sneakers ad only talked about the laces and didn't even mention the great ankle support.

Then explain your idea. Use the clearest words you can to tell exactly what you have in mind. If it will help, draw a picture on another sheet of paper to illustrate what you're talking about (put your name on this paper in case it gets separated from your letter).

At the end of your letter, you should thank the person you're writing to for giving attention to your idea and say you hope the company will consider it seriously. If you want, you can say again how much you like the product. A little praise always makes people think you must know what you're talking about!

Here is a letter Mary Sunshine wrote to the manufacturer of the shampoo she likes to use.

———————

12 S. Maple Ave.
Anyplace, CA 90000
805-555-0000
November 20, 19—

President
Mother Hubbard Co.
2345 Cupboard St.
Dogbone, IL 60000

Dear Sir or Madam:

I really love Mother Hubbard shampoo, and I've been using it for quite a long time. However, I think the bottle it comes in could be improved.

Since the shampoo is so thick, it's hard to get the last of it out of the bottle. I've tried standing the bottle upside down, but it falls over because the top is round. If the top screwed off, I could add a little water to make the last of the shampoo come out. But the top of your bottle doesn't unscrew, it's made so you have to pull it off. This is very hard to do, especially when you're standing in the shower with wet hands.

Another problem is that the shampoo bottle is dark-colored plastic, so you can't see through it. I get very annoyed when it turns out there's not enough left in the bottle for one shampoo. If you made the bottle translucent, it would be easy to see when it was time to buy more.

I hope the Mother Hubbard Company will think seriously about changing the design of the shampoo bottle. Putting the shampoo in bottles that can be seen through and opened easily by your customers would make your shampoo even nicer to use.

Thank you for listening.

Sincerely yours,
Mary Sunshine

Here is the letter Charlie Cool sent to his local television station to explain his idea about their sports news.

2 W. Main St.
Somewhere, NY 10000
914-555-0000
December 1, 19—

President
WSHU-TV
7809 Somany St.
Somewhere, NY 10000

Dear Sir or Madam:

I watch your six o'clock newscast every night because I always want to see what's happening in sports. And I like your sports anchor, Red Baron, because he doesn't make a bunch of dumb jokes like some of the other channels' sports people do. But I have an idea for improving the sports news part of your program.

Instead of having the same old replays of game clips that everyone has already seen, why don't you show how the players practice for the different positions? For instance, I'm playing basketball now in school and I'd like to know what kind of drills professional players use to practice

their plays. You could also show how they practice free throws and show what exercises they do
to keep in shape.

I think a lot of sports fans would like to see the
inside story of how teams get ready for games.
And I think if you showed this sort of thing
instead of replays of games from the day before,
you'd get a lot of new viewers.

I hope you will think about my idea and at
least give it a try.

Yours truly,
Charlie Cool

Companies may have lots of reasons you don't know
about for doing things the way they do. But you'll never
know if your idea was just what they needed to improve
their product or service unless you write to them. So send
off your ideas for improvements and see if you can get
things to change for the better.

12. Opinion Letters ₹✹

Like most people, you probably have opinions about all kinds of things. You may feel strongly about finding ways to save the environment from pollution, or you might believe that there should be stronger laws to protect endangered species. The issues you care about don't have to be such big ones, though. Perhaps you feel it's kind of dangerous to ride a bike in your town, and you think the city council should have special bike lanes painted on the streets. You probably have lots of opinions about the rules in your school, and you might feel that some of them are unnecessary or unfair.

You and your friends may discuss these things from time to time, but does anyone else care what you think? The answer is yes! Anyone who is elected or appointed to make decisions that will affect others really does care what those people think. Hearing from voters can, and often does, change a politician's mind about an issue. You're not a voter yet, but you will be in a few years. Your opinions may be positive or negative, but they matter to the people who are in charge.

Not very many kids write to explain their opinions to

people who make decisions, so your letter will stand out. It will be taken seriously simply because you took the time and trouble to write. If you write to say you agree with what is being done, that lets the person know that his or her decisions are supported by some of the people they affect. If your letter disagrees with some policy, maybe it will help get that policy changed.

Who Should You Write To?

Most opinion letters are written to government officials or elected representatives, because they are generally the people who decide on policies and laws. You can write to anyone from the president of the United States to your local representative in your city or town government.

Try to figure out who might be responsible for making the decision you are concerned about. Sometimes it's hard to tell. For example, obviously the president of the United States isn't involved in deciding whether or not your town has bike lanes. But who is in charge of deciding about big issues like the environment? Local officials may be responsible for some environmental laws, while other policies are made by officials of the federal government in Washington, DC. If you're not sure who to write to, ask your parents or your teacher, or call the office of your town's mayor or your district's congressperson.

For school problems, you may want to write to your principal. Public-school principals are not elected government officials, but they are responsible to the superintendent and to the school board, which is a governmental body.

There is a chain of command involved in almost every

decision about policies and laws. In schools, the principal, the superintendent, and the school board make the decisions. So if your opinion involves only your school, your principal is the first person to write to. He or she may be able to change things or to explain why they shouldn't be changed. If you're not happy with the principal's response to your letter, you may want to move up the chain of command and write to the superintendent and then the school board.

In the same way, if you're dealing with a governmental issue, it's best to start at the right level of government — the one that can really affect the subject you're concerned about. If you don't get a helpful response, you can keep moving up the chain. At the national level, you may want to send several copies of the first letter you write. The president, both of your U.S. senators, and your representative to Congress all deal with national policies. There may be others as well. For example, if your opinion letter is about the environment, it might be a good idea to send a copy to the head of the Environmental Protection Agency too.

How to Find Addresses

Once you've decided on the right level of government, you may need to find the name and address of the person to send your opinion letter to. Some addresses for national policymakers are given in Appendix 2 at the back of this book. But what if you need other kinds of addresses?

Your local telephone book is your best resource. There is an amazing amount of information in most phone books, and it's quite easy to track down the particular names and addresses you need. Check the phone book's table of contents to find the government section. It lists local, county, state, and federal government departments and offices. You can call the listed number to find out the name of the person and the address to send your letter to. If you can't find the department you want, call a general one like "City Hall" or "Board of Supervisors" or "Office of the Superintendent." Or look for a number at the beginning or end of the listings that you can call for information that isn't included. For state and federal information, this will probably be an 800 number, which means your call is free.

Most people who answer the phones at government offices want to be helpful. They'll try to figure out the names of the legislators for the district you live in if you're not sure who they are, or they'll give you another number to call to get the information you want. So don't feel you're imposing on them by making this kind of call — they'll probably be happy to talk to someone who's not sounding off about a problem!

What Should You Say?

When you are writing to someone to tell your opinion about an issue, it's important to say things as clearly as you can. Here are some points to include in your letter.

Explain what the issue is, and what your opinion is about it, in plain language. Make sure your facts are correct — if they are not, much of the impact of your letter is lost.

Explain why the issue concerns you personally. By telling who you are and why you care about whatever it is, you give extra importance to your opinion. You might say you're a student at ABC School or a resident of Nowhereville; this gives a good reason for your concern about a school or town issue. If you want, you can identify yourself in a few words under your typed name at the end of the letter; it might read "Sixth-grade student, XYZ Middle School" or "Member, Clean Skies Committee." It's good to tell who you are when you write your opinion letter on any issue, but you don't have to be a member of an environmental group to write about the environment. You can just write as a citizen of the world who cares about this problem.

Tell the person you're writing to what you want him or her to do. Vote a certain way? Sponsor a new law? Change a school rule? Whatever it is, don't make your letter into a guessing game; explain what you want to happen.

Suppose your school doesn't have a recycling program and you think it should start one. Write to the principal and say you think it is up to him or her to encourage recycling in the school. You could also make specific suggestions for how to do this, such as getting separate trash bins for the lunchroom.

What if your representative to the city council has recently made a speech saying that the law against buses standing for more than two minutes with their engines idling should be enforced? If you feel strongly about this as a way of reducing air and noise pollution, why not write to him or her and say you agree? You could say you heard about the speech on the news and you hope he or she will continue to work against pollution.

Whatever you say in your opinion letters, say it politely. Don't use slang and don't be too casual; remember, this is a business letter and you want it to be taken seriously.

Here are letters Charlie Cool and Mary Sunshine wrote to express their opinions on a number of issues.

2 W. Main St.
Somewhere, NY 10000
914-555-0000

January 5, 19—

The Honorable Polly Flinders
City Councilwoman
City Hall
500 N. Cinders St.
Somewhere, NY 10000

Dear Ms. Flinders:

I read in the newsletter you sent to our house that you are going to suggest a "loose-dog park" for our city. I just wanted to tell you that I think it's a great idea!

I don't own a dog myself right now, but I sometimes walk other people's dogs. There is no place in town where I can let them off the leash to run around. A park like the one you're suggesting, with a fence around it to keep the dogs inside, would make dogs and their owners very happy. It probably would make other people happy too, because they don't like it when dogs run into the street in front of their cars or race across their lawns.

I'm not old enough to vote yet (I'm in middle school), but if I were, I would definitely vote for you in the next election. Please keep supporting the "loose-dog park."

Yours truly,
Charlie Cool

—— ✤ ——

2 W. Main St.
Somewhere, NY 10000
914-555-0000

January 10, 19—

Mr. Simple Simon
Commissioner
Pieman Baseball Program
900 Ware Ave.
Somewhere, NY 10000

Dear Mr. Simon:

I've been meaning to write this letter to you ever since the Pieman baseball season ended. I've played Pieman baseball for three years, and I'd like to give you one player's opinion.

Most kids who play Pieman baseball aren't very good when they first start. I know I barely knew how to hit when I first joined. I had a great coach (Mr. Fair) who taught us all a lot and made everyone enjoy learning and playing. But some of the other coaches of teams we played against were really mean, not just to our team but to their own teams. They made kids cry by yelling at them when they made errors or struck out. We felt really bad for the kids on those teams, and it wasn't much fun to play against them.

In my opinion, the coaches make or break the program for the players. I think as Commissioner of the Pieman Baseball Program, you should tell your coaches not to be so unpleasant. It's supposed to be fun to play Pieman baseball; after all, we're just kids, not major leaguers. When coaches make kids cry, I don't think the kids will want to play anymore.

Thanks for reading this letter. I really do like playing baseball, and I hope the Pieman program will be more fun this season.

Yours truly,
Charlie Cool
3rd Baseman,
Pieman Plates

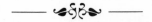

12 S. Maple Ave.
Anyplace, CA 90000
805-555-0000
January 31, 19—

The Honorable Goosey Gander
State Senate Building
1000 Wanderwhere St.
Sacramento, CA 90000

Dear Senator Gander:

I am a student at Anyplace Middle School and I strongly support your efforts to increase our state's spending on education.

My school has good teachers and a good principal, but there are lots of things that would make the school better. We can't use our school library very often, because we don't have a librarian anymore. This makes it hard to use books that aren't actually in our classroom. A couple of classrooms are closed in our school because the roof leaks. The classes have more kids than they used to, because there are fewer teachers. I think this makes it harder to learn.

I've talked to some people in Anyplace about these problems, and they say that each town is supposed to pay for its own schools. They say people in our town are already paying as much as they can. It doesn't seem fair that kids in rich towns have much better schools than kids in poorer areas, but even the schools in rich places need to be better. I think the state should help all communities make their schools as good as possible.

I hope you will keep working for more money for education. And I'd to know what kids can do to help. After all, we're the ones in school right now, so we're the ones who are directly affected by the state's decisions about education. Please let me know if you have ideas about how we can help improve our schools.

Sincerely yours,
Mary Sunshine

No matter what your opinion is on an issue, it's important to write it in a letter. Decision makers can't know what your opinions are unless you tell them. Opinion letters are a good way to make your voice heard.

13. Letters for Publication ॐ

It's really exciting to see something you've written published in your local newspaper or in a magazine. But what kind of letter can you write that anyone would want to publish?

First of all, you might write to express your opinion about something that's been in the news or was in the magazine. For instance, maybe you read a magazine article that told all about a science experiment or craft project that you could do at home. But the project didn't work, even though you followed the directions carefully. This is a good time to write and express your disappointment and your hope that next time they'll provide more accurate instructions. The magazine might publish your letter along with corrections to the instructions.

Your local newspaper probably has a letters column where people can express their views. You can read everything there from angry feelings about local problems to praise for a teacher or a local group. People often write in to correct what they think is an error in a news article. A news reporter may have written that last night's fire was the first one ever at XYZ Company's warehouse, and a reader could point out in a letter that there was a fire there last year. And, of course, there are usually letters for and against various politicians.

These are called letters to the editor, and the editor is the person you send your letter to. You'll find a column of letters from readers in almost every magazine and newspaper; that column will also tell you where to send your letter. While you're looking for the address, take time to read a few of the letters printed there so you can see how other people phrase theirs. Some of them are not very well written, but most of them are short. Newspaper and magazine editors may shorten long letters before they print them.

Letters on many subjects are published in advice columns. Your local paper may carry letters and replies about gardening, home repair, pet care, medical and legal problems, as well as personal advice columns such as "Dear Abby" and "Ask Beth."

People who write advice columns really do get the letters they publish from readers — they don't make them up. So if you have a question that fits the subject of an advice column in a newspaper or magazine you read, why not write and ask it? But don't be surprised if it takes a very long time for it to be published and answered, or even if it doesn't get in the paper at all. Popular advice columnists get thousands of letters every week, and they have space to answer only a few of them.

Another reason you might write to your local newspaper is to announce an event that your school or a group you belong to is having. Many newspapers publish a list once a week of all kinds of events. It might be called

"Calendar" or "What's Happening" or something like that, and it probably includes everything from church bazaars to women's club meetings to school fairs and concerts. Look for that section of your newspaper and use the section's name or title in addressing your announcement letter. Then it will be sure to get to the person who is putting together this list for the paper. Of course, you can always send your announcement to the editor of the newspaper and it will eventually get to the correct department. Be sure to send it in plenty of time — you can call the newspaper to ask how early they need it.

Where to Send Your Letter for Publication

All newspapers and magazines publish their addresses in every issue. You can almost always find the address on page 2 or the editorial page of a newspaper and close to the table of contents of a magazines (don't send your letter to the subscription department).

At the end of most advice columns, often in a little box, you'll usually find the address for letters to the columnist. Sometimes this box also has directions for writing letters for publication. If the column you want to write to doesn't show a special address at the end, you can send your letter to the column at the newspaper's main address.

Mary Sunshine sent a question about repairing her bike to the Ms. Fix-It column in her local newspaper (no special address was listed for the column). Her envelope looked like this.

Mary Sunshine
12 S. Maple Ave.
Anyplace, CA 90000

STAMP

"Ms. Fix-It"
The Anyplace News
Old King Cole Square
Anyplace, CA 90000

What Should You Say?

Since space for letters in newspapers and magazines is
limited, it's best to make your letter short. If it's too long, it
may not be published. And if the editor decides to publish
it anyway, it will probably be cut down to fit into the
available space. So if you don't want some of what you
have to say to be left out, keep your letter brief.

LETTERS TO THE EDITOR

Think through what you want to say in your letter to the
editor. And make sure any facts you use to support your
opinion are really true. Nothing is more embarrassing than
to have your letter published and then to find out from a
friend that you had the facts all wrong.

You'll probably want to write your letter to the editor in
a rough draft and then go over it carefully before you write

the final copy. Don't forget that lots of people who don't know you and may not agree with you will be reading this letter if it is published. Try to imagine how what you write will sound to a stranger who is opening up the morning paper and meeting you for the first time in print.

You want to make the best impression you can. So when you read over your letter, ask yourself some questions. Are the spelling and punctuation correct? Did you get all the facts and details right? Would a stranger reading this understand what you're trying to say? Would he or she think you were making a good point? It's okay to sound angry, but your letter needs to explain the reasons for your anger. And even if you're angry, always be polite. Name calling makes your letter sound babyish.

LETTERS TO ADVICE COLUMNS

In a letter to an advice column, it's important that you explain your problem clearly so that you can get the advice you need. For example, if what you want to know is how to teach your dog to shake hands, you need to say in your letter how old your dog is and what you have already taught it to do. The advice would be different for a two-year-old dog that knows how to sit and stay than for an eight-week-old puppy that isn't even housebroken yet. Again, it's best to keep your letter as short as you can while still including all the necessary information. And of course you'll check to make sure your letter is neat, with proper spelling and punctuation.

LETTERS THAT ANNOUNCE EVENTS

For a letter announcing an event that's coming up, the most important thing is getting all the information down exactly right. If the fair is on Saturday and Sunday and your letter says it's on Sunday only, you'll be disappointed with the turnout on Saturday. And if you give the wrong address, the person who lives at that address may be a little upset when a whole mob shows up at his door. Don't forget to tell who's putting on the event and how much it costs to get in. If it's free, say so.

Look over your letter carefully and double check the date, time, location, and all the other details. Even if your letter is perfect, it's always possible that what's printed in the paper will be wrong. After all, newspapers do sometimes make mistakes. But at least you will have done all you can to get the right information to the readers who want it.

SIGN YOUR LETTER

All letters you write for publication need to have your name and address on them. Newspapers will not publish an unsigned letter to the editor. They want to make sure the letter isn't a fake. It's a good idea to put your phone number on a letter to the editor or an announcement of events. The newspaper may want to call you to make sure the information is correct and that you really are the person who sent the letter.

If your letter to the editor is published, your name will be published as its writer unless you say you don't want it to appear in print. Different newspapers have different policies about publishing "Name Withheld" letters to the editor.

Personal advice columns are different. You've probably noticed that the letters in "Dear Abby" and "Ann Landers" are sometimes signed with names like "Mad in

Mudville." Because the kinds of things people write about to these columns are often embarrassing or very serious, the columnist is willing to shield anyone's identity who asks to remain anonymous.

Here are letters for publication that Charlie Cool and Mary Sunshine wrote.

2 W. Main St.
Somewhere, NY 10000
914-555-0000
February 10, 19—

Editor
The Somewhere Sentinel
100 Sixpence Lane
Somewhere, NY 10000

Dear Editor:

I went to New York City last weekend and I was amazed at how many homeless people I saw there on the streets. I had read about this problem in the papers, but seeing it in person is different. It's terrible to see so many people who have no home to go to and who are begging for money and searching the trash cans for food.

I know it's not just a problem in New York City. This is a big problem all over the country. But that's what makes me mad. How did we let the problem get so big? It seems to me that if we can send money and food to help people in other countries, we can find a way to help people in our own country. I don't understand why people say we don't have the money to do this.

Go and see this for yourself. It will make you really sad. This isn't just a problem in one city or one part of the country. It's a problem we all have together. Maybe if we all start to realize how serious this problem has become in our country, we can work together to find a solution.

Yours truly,
Charlie Cool
Student,
Somewhere Middle
School

—— ❧❧ ——

2 W. Main St.
Somewhere, NY 10000
914-555-0000
February 20, 19—

"Ask Mother Goose"
The Somewhere Sentinel
100 Sixpence Lane
Somewhere, NY 10000

Dear Mother Goose:

I like baby-sitting and I'm pretty good at it. When I sit with little kids, they always tell their parents they want me to come back. But when I talk to new people about baby-sitting, they sometimes act like they think it's weird that a boy wants to baby-sit.

Lots of girls my age baby-sit. Why does anyone think it's strange that a boy would want to work as a baby-sitter too? What can I tell people to convince them that I'm just as serious about this job as girls are?

Please sign me
Confused (Charlie Cool)

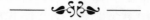

12 S. Maple Ave.
Anyplace, CA 90000
805-555-0000
February 25, 19—

"This Week's Events"
The Anyplace News
Old King Cole Square
Anyplace, CA 90000

Dear Sir or Madam:

Ms. Merry Soul's class of the Anyplace Middle School is having a bake sale on March 15, 19—, to raise money to help pay for the class trip to Sacramento this spring.

The bake sale will be held in the south parking lot of Anyplace Middle School, 3 Fiddlers Lane, on Saturday, March 15, from 10 A.M. until 1 P.M.

There will be lots of great goodies made by students and parents. We hope everyone will come and buy something.

Thank you.

Sincerely yours,
Mary Sunshine

No matter whether it's a letter to the editor with your name at the bottom, a question to an advice column with a funny phony name instead of your own, or an announcement of an event with no one's name attached to it at all, seeing something you've written in print is really pretty amazing. So do your best work in putting your opinions, questions, and information down on paper and see if you can become a published writer!

14. Sincerely Yours 🖎

Remember the letter that Mary Sunshine wrote to State Senator Goosey Gander about getting more money to make schools better (see page 132)? Senator Gander was very impressed with Mary's letter. Here's what he wrote back to her.

SENATOR GOOSEY GANDER
State Senate Building
1000 Wanderwhere St.
Sacramento, CA 90000
916-555-0000

March 4, 19—

Miss Mary Sunshine
12 S. Maple Ave.
Anyplace, CA 90000

Dear Miss Sunshine:

Thank you for your thoughtful letter about the need for more funding for education. As you know, it's a problem I'm very concerned about, but it's not an easy one to solve.

I was very pleased and impressed with your question about what children can do to help make schools better. I hope you don't mind that I showed your letter to several of my colleagues in the State Senate, and they too believe that participation by students in improving education is a terrific idea. We will be giving the idea a lot of thought and will let you know how we feel you and your friends could best contribute.

In the meantime, I have a suggestion. Why don't you send your letter to your local newspaper for publication? I would like to see more young people like you get involved in issues that concern all of us.

Thank you again for writing to me. I'll keep you informed of our progress toward the goal of making schools better.

Sincerely yours,
Goosey Gander

Mary thought that Senator Gander's idea of sending her letter to the newspaper made a lot of sense. Luckily, she had kept a copy of the letter, so she sent it to *The Anyplace News*. Along with it, she sent a letter to the editor explaining that this was a copy of her letter to Senator Gander.

The Anyplace News published Mary Sunshine's letter in the "Letters to the Editor" column about a week later. Lots of people called her to tell her they thought it was a great letter, and they too wanted to get involved in making schools better. Mary was pretty excited that her letter had been read by so many people.

The next thing that happened was even more exciting.

The large corporation that owned *The Anyplace News* decided to reprint Mary's letter in the other newspapers it owned all over the country. The head of the corporation thought that lots of people would be interested in reading a young person's letter about schools and education.

One of the newspapers that published Mary's letter was *The Somewhere Sentinel.* Charlie Cool had been reading the "Letters to the Editor" column in the *Sentinel* ever since he had sent in his own letter about homeless people. When his letter was published, he felt really good. He kept reading the letters column to see if anyone would write a letter in response to his.

When Mary Sunshine's letter was published, Charlie Cool read it. He thought it was pretty neat that a letter from a kid in California had appeared in a newspaper in New York. Mary's letter made Charlie start thinking about the problems in his own school. After a while, he decided to write Mary a letter. As you can see, he didn't think he needed to use a business letter format.

> 2 W. Main St.
> Somewhere, NY 10000
> March 15, 19—

Dear Mary Sunshine,

 I read your letter about schools in *The Somewhere Sentinel* — did you know it got published in a New York newspaper? Anyway, I wanted to tell you that I thought your letter was great. I'm in middle school too, and it seems like there's never enough money for all the stuff we need to do. This year there's only one bus to take kids to school, so it has to make two trips in the morning and two in the afternoon. You can imagine how much fun it is to get up a whole hour earlier if you're assigned to the early bus route!

Do you think there is really any way that kids like us could make a difference? I'd like to help, but I don't know where to start. Please write back and tell me if you have any ideas of what kids could do. There are lots of kids here that would help.

Yours truly,
Charlie Cool

After he wrote his letter, Charlie realized that he didn't know Mary Sunshine's address. He knew she lived in Anyplace, California, because when her letter was published in his newspaper, it said it had first appeared in *The Anyplace News*.

Finally he figured that the best thing to do was to send his letter to Mary Sunshine in care of *The Anyplace News*. In the reference room at the library, he found the newspaper's address in a big book called the *Gale Directory of Publications and Broadcast Media*.

Charlie put his letter to Mary in an envelope with her name on the front. He sealed the envelope and added a stamp. Then he wrote a short letter to the editor of *The Anyplace News*.

---

2 W. Main St.
Somewhere, NY 10000
March 15, 19—

Editor
The Anyplace News
Old King Cole Square
Anyplace, CA 90000

Dear Sir or Madam:

I have enclosed a letter to Mary Sunshine, whose letter to Senator Gander about schools appeared in your newspaper last month. I hope you will be able to forward it to her, because I don't know her address. Thank you.

Yours truly,
Charlie Cool

Charlie put this letter and the envelope addressed to Mary Sunshine in another envelope and sent it to *The Anyplace News*. (You don't have to do it this way if you're writing to an author, for example, in care of his or her publisher — the publisher will recognize the author's name and forward the letter. But Charlie was afraid the people at the newspaper wouldn't know who Mary Sunshine was, so he wanted to remind them.)

When Mary got Charlie's letter, she was thrilled. She had never imagined that her letter to Senator Gander would find her a new friend on the other side of the country. But then she realized that a letter can be a powerful way of communicating.

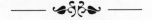

When you think about it, there are lots of ways your letters can touch other people's lives. They can make a sick friend feel more cheerful or can let someone know he or she is appreciated. They can bring comfort to someone who's feeling sad or tell a friend you're proud of him or her. Letters can also reach out to foreign lands, find you information, right a wrong, or let your voice be heard. Your letters can change the world. All you need to do is write them.

Appendices ☙
Index ☙

Appendix 1. Addressing Envelopes

The U.S. Postal Service prefers that everyone use standard two-letter abbreviations for the names of states in the addresses and return addresses on envelopes. Most people now use these same abbreviations in return addresses and inside addresses on the letter itself.

Here are the standard state abbreviations recommended by the Postal Service. Notice that only capital letters are used and there is no punctuation.

AL	Alabama	ID	Idaho
AK	Alaska	IL	Illinois
AZ	Arizona	IN	Indiana
AR	Arkansas	IA	Iowa
CA	California	KS	Kansas
CO	Colorado	KY	Kentucky
CT	Connecticut	LA	Louisiana
DE	Delaware	ME	Maine
DC	District of Columbia	MD	Maryland
FL	Florida	MA	Massachusetts
GA	Georgia	MI	Michigan
HI	Hawaii	MN	Minnesota

MS	Mississippi	RI	Rhode Island
MO	Missouri	SC	South Carolina
MT	Montana	SD	South Dakota
NE	Nebraska	TN	Tennessee
NV	Nevada	TX	Texas
NH	New Hampshire	UT	Utah
NJ	New Jersey	VT	Vermont
NM	New Mexico	VA	Virginia
NY	New York	WA	Washington
NC	North Carolina	WV	West Virginia
ND	North Dakota	WI	Wisconsin
OH	Ohio	WY	Wyoming
OK	Oklahoma		
OR	Oregon	PR	Puerto Rico
PA	Pennsylvania	VI	Virgin Islands

In Canada, too, standard two-letter abbreviations are preferred for the names of provinces. Here are the correct ones to use:

AB	Alberta	NT	Northwest Territories
BC	British Columbia	ON	Ontario
LB	Labrador	PE	Prince Edward Island
MB	Manitoba	QC	(or PQ) Quebec
NB	New Brunswick	SK	Saskatchewan
NF	Newfoundland	YT	Yukon
NS	Nova Scotia		

You should spell out the whole name of any city, unless it's always abbreviated (as in St. Paul or St. Louis).

If you don't know the ZIP code for the address on your letter, you can look it up in the ZIP Code directory at any post office. First look up the state, then under it the city (they are arranged alphabetically). In large cities, you might have to look up the street name to get the right ZIP code. It's kind of a pain to do this sometimes, but it will help your letter get where it's going faster. And when you find the ZIP code, write it down so you'll have it the next time you write to that person!

The Postal Service recommends that addresses on envelopes be typed using all capital letters and no punctuation. You'll see that a lot of the junk mail that comes to your house is addressed this way by computers. But it looks very weird, especially in handwriting, to use no punctuation at all, and the rule is really meant for large businesses that mail thousands of letters each day. If your envelopes are addressed clearly and neatly, your letters will get to their destinations.

The Postal Service has standard abbreviations to be used for words like Street, Avenue, Road, and so on. Here are a few of the most common ones; you can get a complete list if you want one from any post office.

AVE	Avenue	PL	Place
BLVD	Boulevard	PLZ	Plaza
CYN	Canyon	RD	Road
CIR	Circle	SQ	Square
CT	Court	ST	Street
DR	Drive	STA	Station
GDNS	Gardens	TER	Terrace
HWY	Highway	TRL	Trail
IS	Island	TPKE	Turnpike
LN	Lane	WALK	Walk
MDWS	Meadows	WAY	Way
PKY	Parkway		

Other abbreviations are directions; you can probably figure out what N, E, S, W, NE, SE, NW, and SW stand for.

If you need to write an address that has a post office box number or a rural route number, here's how the Postal Service wants them to look:

PO BOX 1234

RR 5   BOX 6

If you are sending a letter to a foreign country, put the name of the country in all capitals on the last line of the address.

Other countries use postal codes that are different from U.S. ZIP codes, so write the address the way it's written on the other person's return address. Otherwise the post office in the other country might not know where the letter is going. And remember that mail to other countries costs more to send than mail inside the United States. You'll probably want to take a letter that's going outside the U.S. to the post office to get the right kind of stamp for it.

Appendix 2. Forms of Address

For most letters, it's pretty clear what titles to use and how to write the greeting for people you're writing to. But there are some special cases, such as the president of the United States, that traditionally need special titles and greetings. These are called "forms of address," and it's polite to use them if you are writing to these people. (You can find a complete list of forms of address at the back of many dictionaries.) The street addresses given here are the correct ones for these officials, but you'll have to look up their real names.

THE PRESIDENT

The President
The White House
Washington, DC 20500

Dear President Winkie: or
Dear Mr. (or Ms.) President:

THE VICE-PRESIDENT

The Vice-President
Old Executive Office Building
17th St. and Pennsylvania Ave.
Washington, DC 20501

Dear Vice-President Grundy: or
Dear Ms. (or Mr.) Vice-President:

U.S. SENATOR

The Honorable Daffy Downdilly
United States Senator
Senate Office Building
Washington, DC 20510

Dear Senator Downdilly:

U.S. REPRESENTATIVE

The Honorable Robin Redbreast
House of Representatives
Rayburn Building
Washington, DC 20515

Dear Representative Redbreast:

GOVERNOR

The Honorable Marjorie Daw
Governor of Statename
State Capitol
Capitalcity, XX 00000

Dear Governor Daw:

MAYOR

The Honorable Tommy Snooks
Mayor of Cityname
City Hall
Cityname, XX 00000
Dear Mayor Snooks:

As a general rule, the envelope and the inside address should use "The Honorable" for most elected officials and high appointed officials: for U.S. senators, representatives, ambassadors, and cabinet members; for governors, state senators, and state representatives; for mayors, aldermen, and county clerks.

All judges are also addressed as "The Honorable," except for justices of the U.S. Supreme Court. For them, address your letters to either "The Chief Justice of the United States" or, for the others, "Ms. Justice Blue." The greeting is either "Dear Mr. (or Ms.) Chief Justice" or "Dear Justice Blue."

What if you're writing to religious leaders? Here are some of the correct forms of address.

	ENVELOPE	GREETING
Rabbi	Rabbi Thomas Green	Dear Rabbi Green:
Catholic Priest	The Reverend Tom Tinker	Dear Father Tinker:
Protestant Minister	The Reverend Jenny Wren	Dear Ms. Wren:

Although it's polite to use these fancy titles and forms of address, it's not the end of the world if you don't do it exactly right. Just try to use their correct titles and names, so your letters will reach the right people.

Appendix 3. Pen Pals

Do you think it would be fun to have a pen pal from another city or state or even another country? There are several organizations listed below that help kids find pen pals. You can write to them and tell them your age, your special hobbies or interests, and whether you want to write to a boy or a girl. Most of them charge a small fee for this service. Also, many pen pal organizations give discounts if more than one person signs up. Perhaps your whole class at school or your Scout troop or just a bunch of friends would like to get pen pals.

International Pen Friends
PO Box 2409
Monroe, MI 48161

International Youth Service
PB 125, SF-20101
Turku 10
FINLAND

League of Friendship, Inc.
PO Box 509
Mount Vernon, OH 43050

Student Letter Exchange
RFD #4
Waseca, MN 56093

World Pen Pals
1694 Como Ave.
St. Paul, MN 55108

Another way to find pen pals is in magazines, especially the ones that are about particular hobbies or that focus on special interests. Many such magazines publish lists of people in various age groups who want to find new pen pals. Just look through the list and pick out someone who sounds like your kind of person.

Index 𑁋